Life Song

Life Song

IN HARMONY WITH ALL CREATION

By Bill Schul, Ph.D.

STILLPOINT PUBLISHING

STILLPOINT PUBLISHING
Building a society that honors The Earth,
Humanity, and The Sacred in All Life.

For a free catalog or ordering information, write
Stillpoint Publishing, Box 640, Walpole, NH 03608, USA
or call
1-800-847-4014 TOLL FREE (Continental US, except NH)
1-603-756-9281 (Foreign and NH)

This book is manufactured in the United States of America.

Cover design by Karen Savary
Text & layout by Sally Nichols

Published by Stillpoint Publishing, Box 640,
Meetinghouse Road, Walpole, NH 03680

ISBN 1-883478-01-4

Schul, Bill. *Life Song: In Harmony with All Creation*
Library of Congress Number 94-67880

1 3 5 7 9 8 6 4 2

This book is printed on chlorine-free recycled paper
to save trees and preserve Earth's ecology.

Dedication

*To those persons whose hearts are large enough
to embrace all living creatures and whose minds are
wise enough to understand the importance of human
sharing with all God's creatures.*

Contents

Foreword

The physical plane offers opportunities for Spirit to express different qualities through a myriad of life forms. All forms are important as reflections of divine essence. All individuals of whatever species, from bacteria to whales, deserve reverence as manifestations of infinite creativity.

In the dance of life on planet Earth, humans have experimented with many ways of living and many philosophies, exploring the limits of their capacities for creation and destruction. It seems that modern western industrialized humanity has taken the game of focusing on material acquisition and controlling or "conquering" nature as far as it can go. Unfortunately, denying the spiritual quality of all life around us has brought disease and destruction for our ecosystem and its members, including our own species. We have been so successful in applying the philosophy of domination that it is killing us.

Human society seems to have a built-in inertia that addresses the need to radically change our habituated ways only when at the brink of cataclysm. Rational foresight of consequences seems to be a rare quality of usually unheeded individuals rather than a common human inheritance. Fortunately, growing numbers of people now see the need for a different approach to life—a philosophy that includes all of life as important and integral to our well-being, and sees us as a part of nature rather than separate from or above it.

Many people long for a restoration of spiritual oneness, a recognition that all life is not only important for our well-being, but that we are part of it in a sacred, essential way. The native ways, decimated by the onrush of western colonization, are being recalled for their success in living in harmony with nature. We are reviving deep memories of other times and places when humans revered all of life around them and felt how integral this connection was to their physical, emotional, and spiritual destiny.

Many are seeking the restoration of ancient abilities to understand all living beings—to hear their song as intimately as a deep conversation with a friend. Stellar individuals throughout the ages have communicated mind-to-mind and heart-to-heart with animals, plants, and the elements of the Earth. The results have been extraordinary cooperation and displays of intelligence and compassion from other species towards humans, striking deep chords in the soul. Most of us were taught to renounce the direct communication that was natural to us as children, when our hearts were open, as childish and unreasonable flights of imagination. We long for our wounded separation to be healed. We are tired of the psychological barriers and alienation that create despair and dis-ease. We want to be free as children and close to the Earth, each other and ourselves again. We long to return to wholeness.

In Life Song, Bill Schul gives us hope. Through rich stories of interspecies communication and the positive result they bring to all involved, we are moved to reach inward to find that still-burning ember of connection that will show us the way to understand others of any species. The discoveries of fellow human beings invite us to take the leap ourselves, to bridge the gap we have allowed our socialization to impose. The rewards are increased joy, harmony, and wisdom. Read about the exciting possibilities, and may you never be the same!

— Penelope Smith,
Animal Communication Specialist

PUBLISHER'S NOTE

Penelope Smith is the author of:
Animal Talk: Interspecies Telepathic Communication
Animals: Our Return to Wholeness
The Interspecies Telepathic Communication Tape Series
Animal Death: A Spiritual Journey
and editor of *Species Link* (Quarterly Journal).

Acknowledgments

My deepest thanks to those persons who contributed to the research involved in writing *Life Song*, and to those interviewed in the field of human-animal communications as well as those who have dug a little deeper in the soil of the plant kingdom. Thanks to those creatures, large and small, with whom I have shared my life, and to those persons I have known whose gifts of communicating with various expressions of life have endowed my own so richly.

I wish to express my appreciation to my publishers, Errol Sowers and Meredith Young-Sowers, for their faith in this book, and my editors, Dorothy Seymour and Ann Weil Richards, whose critical faculties improved the manuscript substantially.

My special thanks to Kent and Terry Comfort for their many hours of computer work as well as their encouragement throughout this project.

Introduction

Recalling the many hours spent as a boy with my shepherd, Curly, wandering through the woods and along Possey Creek, I wonder how my life would have been different without him. Remembering my joy as a youngster poring over the seed catalogues that always arrived in abundance each Spring, I try to fathom how life would have been other than on the farm. And I ask myself: how would I describe life without the lessons of so many teachers, human and otherwise?

These questions cannot be answered, of course, but I am grateful that they were there on the path with me. My journey, I'm certain, was the richer for it. And I am equally sure that the value of the journey ahead will depend largely on how well my fellow travelers and I listen to one another.

In our expanding universe, all of life's expressions, from a blade of grass to the eagle flying overhead, may be playing roles we have yet to discover. Perhaps our own voices are not the only ones worth listening to, and those of other life forms are of value equal to ours.

In earlier times and among indigenous people, it was common to be attuned to all life's expressions: birds, animals, insects, the trees, the wind. These people understood the inseparable nature of all forms of life and the unity of creation. They were able to integrate themselves with the universal life-force present in every being and everything. Life to them was an all-inclusive relationship in which nothing was meaningless, nothing unimportant, and from which nothing could be excluded. Experiencing this oneness, they extablished no barriers between mineral and vegetable, between vegetable and man, between man and the Great Spirit in which all life existed. They experienced all living things as partners in a universal endeavor. Each member of every species had an individual contribution to make to the general good of all, and only it could supply this. Everything lived for everything else.

It may be possible for us today to recapture this level of interspecies communication. If we did, it could change our lives. We might respond differently to the problems we face with the environment. And we would certainly change our treatment of other creatures.

Life Song

1
Talking with Animals

Most of us talk to animals. Children chatter away at their pets and have no trouble at all believing that their cats, dogs, parakeets, and goldfish have full comprehension. We still talk to our animal friends when we grow older, and we allow that any deficiency they have in handling our language is more than compensated for by their love and loyalty. Anyway, animals are tolerant and un-opinionated sounding boards.

Although we talk to animals, few of us listen to the animals in return. Therein resides the difference between someone who keeps pets and another who develops a profound sharing relationship with an animal. Interspecies communication can evolve only from that sharing relationship.

I have personally known humans who could carry on silent two-way conversations with animals and really share ideas with them. Most of these persons have been

Native Americans, most likely because indigenous peoples have remained attuned to nature.

Mojave Dan and Fred Kimball are two of the most successful in interspecies communication. Dan and Fred knew what animals were thinking and communicated their thoughts to humans.

Mojave Dan was a desert dweller who had learned to listen. He did not live alone; his family consisted of an assortment of burros, dogs, and various wild animals that would remain as members for a while and then move on. The family roamed the desert, and Mojave Dan set up his tent and equipment in a spot and stayed until he became restless. He panned gold, but only enough to pay for supplies.

Mojave Dan didn't read books, magazines, or newspapers, never listened to the radio, never watched television, and seldom asked questions of other humans. Yet he was amazingly well-informed at all time about practically everything that interested him. J. Allen Boone, in his book, *Kinship with All Life,* says Dan's information came from his dogs and burros, from wild animals, from snakes, from insects, from birds— indeed, from almost everything that crossed his trail. "The real mystery," says Boone, "was not so much Dan's ability to silently communicate his thoughts to the animal but his capacity to understand when the animal spoke to him."

Boone was never able to get Mojave Dan to tell him how he was able to accomplish his correspondence with other creatures. His only response was that such things were too intimate to talk about and could be acquired only through personal effort and real humility.

But Boone relates that on a particular occasion he

managed to track down Mojave Dan in order to ask him about his own relationship with a German shepherd named Strongheart. Hours went by, and the desert dweller didn't answer Boone's question. Boone and Mojave Dan fixed their meal, cleaned the pans, and lay on their backs, silently studying the stars in the night sky. Then Mojave Dan finally said, as though aiming his thoughts at the stars, "There's facts about dogs and there's opinions about them. The dogs have the facts, and the humans have the opinions. If you want facts about a dog, always get them straight from the dog. If you want opinions, get them from the human." Having spoken thus, Dan rolled over on his side and went to sleep.

Fred Kimball has been listening for more than fifty years. As a result of this talent, he has located thousands of lost pets, diagnosed physical ailments that eluded the skills of veterinarians, and discovered the nature of emotional and mental stress that caused animals to be depressed, act up, run away, or simply refuse to eat. As with Mojave Dan, Kimball goes to the creatures themselves for answers.

The demand for Kimball's services becomes obvious when one attempts to reach him at his home in Idyllwild, California. Calls to him are picked up by an answering machine. He told me recently that he received so many calls from pet owners that he decided he'd have to record the calls and return them in order.

Kimball's popularity has grown from his accuracy at locating animals and at learning what troubles them. Twice I myself used Kimball's assistance. When I first called Kimball, he suggested that I test his abilities by permitting him to describe my own pet. I agreed.

Without seeing my dog or having me describe her, Kimball announced, "You have a fat little dog there."

I responded that he was right—an overfed basset. He said that Sady was very observant of everything going on around her, that she was telling him I had a limp, and that she was worried about this. I started to deny this, but then I remembered that I had been favoring a foot after stepping on a nail.

Kimball went on, "Sady also says there is an older man there who has trouble with his neck."

That remark startled me. It obviously referred to my father, whom I had been taking to the chiropractor for several weeks because of neck problems. Sady then relayed several other bits of accurate information to Kimball, including being scolded for stealing a cake off the kitchen table. One could claim that he was simply reading my mind, except for the fact that Sady also told Kimball where she had hidden a toy (under the carpet in her doghouse), and I didn't know it was there until I checked.

Later, I called Kimball again, because one evening Sady didn't return home from her jaunt in the nearby fields and woods. We looked for her but couldn't find her. When total darkness set in, we were convinced that Sady was in trouble or had been stolen. She had never been gone this long. When I called Kimball and told him what had happened, after a minute or so he said that Sady was in an open field not far north of three white buildings. He said that Sady informed him that she was very tired and would come home after she was rested. We drove around the area for a while but couldn't locate any small white buildings.

The following morning we started out again, and

when we saw our neighbor's three white fuel storage tanks, we decided that these must have been what Sady had transmitted to Kimball as buildings. There, not more than a hundred yards north of the tanks, we found Sady. She was dead. Apparently, while she was running about the fields, her heart gave out on her. She was lying on the ground as though in sleep.

We have come to accept telepathic exchange between people, but eyebrows usually rise when someone hints that a two-footed creature and a four-footed one have been carrying on a conversation. For some reason we find it easier to accept the idea that animals know what we are thinking than the reverse. It is not at all unusual for pet lovers to tell how their dogs or cats know ahead of time that they are planning a hike in the woods or to leave town for a few days. We marvel at these abilities, accept them as being real enough, and yet, without noticing our contradictions, we are reluctant to admit that the animal must have the equipment to perform these acts.

Fred Kimball has been behaving for many years as though animals have consciousness, and this acceptance has provided him with some lively dialogues with all kinds of furry and feathered conversationalists in many parts of the world. Fred tunes in on animals' thoughts, lets them know he would like to converse with them, and then, if they do—for sometimes they don't—they will tell him about their likes and dislikes and about the people and other animals in their lives.

Sometimes they voice complaints or register some request with Kimball. Once, for example, a horse was being treated for lameness in its hindquarters. The condition was getting worse despite the efforts of several excellent veterinarians. In desperation, the owners asked Kimball to inquire of the horse what was wrong with him.

"I backed into a rough board in my stable and drove a splinter into my spinal column," the horse communicated to the psychic. This information was referred to a veterinarian, and close examination revealed the splinter, which was removed, and the horse got well.

One might say that Kimball is a pet consultant. He is a nationally known psychic who has appeared on network television and radio shows and has been interviewed by many newspapers, and he lectures widely in this and other countries.

So what else is odd about Fred Kimball? Has he lived in a cave or a treehouse most of his life, learning to howl and to warble? No, it hasn't been necessary for him to live with animals in the wild or try to imitate their sounds. His communication is on the level of mental images; verbal exchange is unnecessary.

Curiously, as a child Kimball was not clairaudient. At age nine, however, he became interested in hypnotism and for a time performed as a carnival hypnotist. He gave up hypnotism as a practice when he was 39, but he credits it with helping him to develop his psychic powers.

Kimball was past forty when he first understood what animals were saying. He was standing sentinel on the deck of a tanker and was watching the flight of a seagull as it glided across the bow of the ship. The graceful bird soared skyward, then reversed its flight and winged its way starboard. As it glided closer to the sailor, it called out, "Hi, Fred!"

"I thought I had been at sea too long when that happened," he told me with a craggy grin. "At first I was sure someone had called my name. I looked around. No one was there. The greeting came again. Surely, someone was calling to me! Again I looked around, but I was alone, and as the graceful bird soared above me I began to realize I was picking up the seagull's thought waves."

For a time Kimball worked with the late Dr. Nandor Fodor, one of New York's foremost psychiatrists and an early researcher in extrasensory perception. It was during this period that Fred experienced his first two-way communication with an animal. Between sessions with Dr. Fodor, Kimball spent a lot of time observing the animals at the Central Park Zoo, studying their habits and movements. One day he was watching a lion. The animal kept pacing his cage in an animated fashion, and Kimball sensed that something was wrong.

"I tried putting myself in tune with his thought waves, and I asked him what he was thinking about."

"Sex!" the lion responded.

"I went to the caretaker and asked why the lion was so obsessed with sex. 'He should be,' the caretaker replied. 'The lioness in the next cage is in heat.'"

Communicating with animals is not easy, according to Kimball, because they have very limited vocabularies. They communicate through images. They send pictures that Kimball sees in his mind and interprets. He voices his questions simply and holds a mental vision of what he is saying. The animal flashes back a mental picture; Kimball translates it into words and relays the information to the pet's owner, trainer, or whoever is involved.

At times, however, Kimball gets the distinct impression of words. Explaining this, he said, "If you were to see a horrible car accident, with blood and bodies all about, you might say something to the effect, 'That's horrible.' In other words, I get a distinct emotional impression that can easily be translated into a simple vocabulary."

Kimball's mind has become so adapted to animals that once when a fellow psychic tuned in on his mind, Kimball got mixed up: "I thought it was a dog talking," he grins.

Once a woman called Kimball and asked if he would "read" her pet dog, who had suddenly taken to soiling the rug. When he did, Kimball says, the dog told him that the woman had just gotten a divorce, that the dog loved the husband and believed the divorce was the woman's fault. The dog told Fred, "She evacuated him, and I am evacuating on the rug." The dog added that he hated the woman and did not want to be with her any longer.

Kimball questioned the woman and asked her if she had recently become divorced. Somewhat startled, she answered that she had. He relayed the dog's message and suggested that she find the pet another home, since the animal had no intention of changing his behavior.

Another time Kimball interviewed some monkeys owned by Mae West, the actress. One of the monkeys told Kimball about a visitor who had watched them playing, and he said gleefully, "I turned the water on him!" Fred thought the monkey meant he had turned a water hose on the visitor. But the actress explained that the monkey had hooked his tail about a pail of water standing nearby, drawn it into the cage, and then thrown the whole thing into the face of her chagrined visitor.

One evening Kimball was invited to the home of Dr.

Gina Cerminara, a psychologist, along with sixteen others who were interested in his work. Several brought their pets for readings, and the animals were kept in their cars until their turns.

Kimball first tried to talk to a German shepherd named Jack who, according to Cerminara, was too excited because of the crowd and wouldn't settle down. The only thing that Kimball was able to get from the dog was that he would die in six months. Later, Jack's owners verified the dog's death within the predicted time.

Duchess, also a German shepherd, told Kimball that she enjoyed riding in the family's white station wagon and sticking her nose out the window on the left side of the front seat, resting her head on the driver's neck. She had a close attachment to the husband but thought the children were nuisances. The owners confirmed the details.

A small mongrel dog told Kimball where he lived and described his surroundings, and then he mentioned that he liked to sleep on a leather-covered couch in a room next to the bathroom. The dog also related that a little girl who lived there, whenever she got upset, would go into the bathroom, sit underneath the water basin, and cry her heart out. The dog said that he became very unhappy whenever this happened. The owner of the dog, quite amazed, stated that all this was true.

The session in Dr. Cerminara's home included talks with a French poodle that felt neglected and unloved and a cat that caught most of the lectures at the Theosophical Society Lodge next door to where it lived. Apparently, the evening was quite successful. The psychologist pointed out that Kimball's work showed that clairaudience applied to communication with other species as well as exchanges between humans.

I have several times used Kimball's talents. He has diagnosed sick horses for me and located lost dogs. I have never been disappointed. Nor have the friends of mine who sought out his services.

What seems to me to be so exciting is the information Kimball provides concerning the inner world of animals. Those who are close to their pets find it valuable to know what the animals are feeling and thinking but often believe the pets cannot convey this information to humans. This view may be as much our limitation as it is the animal's. Kimball and his work help us to realize that wherever there is life there is consciousness. From her experiences, Dr. Cerminara is convinced that animals are endowed with a sensitive psychological awareness comparable to our own, and that they possess "an acute faculty for judgment and appraisal that we ordinarily do not think about because it does not manifest itself in human speech."

Several years ago in Silver City, New Mexico, Kimball encountered an unusual dog. While waiting for a friend who worked at the St. John's mine, Kimball sat down on a cable spool. He soon noticed a large golden-haired dog coming toward him. Kimball observed a great deal of red in the aura about the dog's head and recognized this aura as indicative of an affliction about the head. He patted the dog and commented, "You must be a good fighter." The dog said that he had been, then turned and disappeared into a nearby tunnel. A few seconds later Kimball heard a short bark, and he received a mental picture of the dog tumbling headlong down a shaft, striking his head on something at the bottom and lying still.

Kimball quickly fetched the mine foreman. They

found that the dog had entered a newly-opened section of the mine and fallen down a 45-foot shaft. The foreman said that the dog was blind (thus explaining the red aura), and Kimball saw that the dog relied on his sense of smell to get around. Because this section of the mine was new, the dog had no way of knowing about the open shaft.

The miners were able to lift the unconscious dog from the shaft and decided that it would be merciful to shoot him. Kimball, however, was tuned in mentally with the animal and asked, "Are you going to die?"

The reply came back, "Not unless you kill me." Kimball gave the dog's message to the miners, and they decided to try to nurse him back to health. In a short time the blind dog recovered.

Kimball believes that German shepherds are the most intelligent and fearless canines. "These large animals feel they can kill anything, and they aren't afraid of anyone. Actually, intelligence is not the exclusive property of any breed or species," Kimball says, "but for some reason or other I have run on to more intelligent German shepherds than any other kind of dog. The little dogs are the insecure ones, and they often tell me, 'I risk my life every time I go outside.'" He feels that this fear may have a great deal to do with the nervous temperament of small dogs.

The manner in which Kimball determines the intelligence of an animal is its ability to create mental pictures. He disagrees with the commonly-held belief that dogs are colorblind. "Intelligent dogs convey colors quite easily," he asserts. "Animals of lesser intelligence are not as aware of colors."

Cats are secretive and likely to be less communicative than dogs, Kimball claims. One of the most intelligent creatures he ever talked with was a fourteen-year-old duck by the name of Mrs. Quacker. The duck described her owner's health problems in some detail, and his wife confirmed the diagnosis.

Animals do not normally have large vocabularies, according to Kimball. One dog, for example, told him that she enjoyed chasing "stinking cats," which was her way of describing skunks.

"Animals reflect to a large degree what they see in the people around them," the clairaudient explained. "During one demonstration that I gave in Hollywood I could barely hear a hamster. I asked him why he was talking so low, and the little creature said, 'The old woman in the house won't let anyone talk very loud. She doesn't like noises.' I discovered that the old woman referred to was the grandmother of the family." She was sitting in the audience that day and was quite taken aback that the hamster had the nerve to confront her in that manner, but she did admit that what he communicated to Fred was true.

A seven-year-old cocker spaniel named Gypsy told Kimball that she had come to the session in a dark green car. She described her house and listed the members of the family by name. She was confused, though, when describing the girlfriend of one of the sons: the spaniel thought the girl lived at the house because she opened the refrigerator door so often! Gypsy also told Kimball that her leg had been broken and that it had been patched with permanent wires.

Kimball twice summoned a gopher out of its hole in Harmony Park to feed it, but when a curious youngster got too close, the animal excused himself, saying, "I don't trust that boy," and disappeared into his hole.

Snakes, leopards, pigs, lizards, and tigers have sent out their vibrations to the man who can understand them. Kimball at one time even tuned in on a can of earthworms. "They said they had come from the right side of the building and that there were five of them in the can. A search for the hole and a count of the worms proved this to be the case."

On a recent visit to the mountains, Fred encountered a mounted deer's head. He had the impression that the deer smiled at him, so he concentrated on it. "At first I was saddened that the poor animal had been shot, but then I conjured up a picture of the Donner party, which had been lost in the high country. Once I generated rapport with the deer, I learned the animal had been shot to provide meat for a group of starving people who were living in an old mining tunnel in the Colorado Rockies. The deer indicated that it was not saddened because of the way it had given its life."

Kimball also found that he had a skill many would enjoy. After talking to the entries in a horse race, he picked fourteen of the seventeen winners. Fortunately for the race tracks, however, he does not take advantage of his unusual talents.

While he prefers to be in personal contact with animals, Kimball can communicate with animals, as well as people, through telepathy. He exercises this side of his talent when people call him long distance for readings on their pets, usually involving some pet health problem or loss of a pet. In the latter instance, he tries to tune in on the animal and, when he comes in contact with it, asks the lost animal to describe its surroundings. Through this method he is sometimes able to identify the location well enough so that the animal can be found.

While talking to a friend I elicited the response, "He sounds as though he were quite accomplished, but he isn't the only one who talks to animals."

"Oh, I know," I replied. "We all do to some extent, I suppose."

My friend responded by telling me about another highly attuned communicator, Beatrice Lydecker. "She is a well-known personality who does much the same thing as Kimball. She has been on a number of network television shows," my friend stated.

When I asked Kimball about her, he said, "Sure, Beatrice Lydecker is a good friend of mine. She does a fine job of communicating with animals."

Kimball explained that Beatrice Lydecker had heard him on a radio talk show and, immediately interested in pursuing communication with animals, she read his training book and arranged some time with him. He was amazed how quickly she learned. "She is definitely a person attuned to nature," he said.

When Lydecker was young she planned on becoming a missionary to orphaned children. One day while teaching in California, her attention was drawn to a large German shepherd locked in a yard, and she experienced the sensation that the animal was trying to communicate with her. She approached the dog and suddenly knew what he was thinking and feeling. He told her he was sad because he was left alone so much of the time. She located the dog's owner and learned that he had been injured some months before and had bought the dog for company. When he became well enough to work again, he left the dog by himself all during the day, and the dog felt lonesome.

Messages from animals continued to come through to Lydecker. The unexpected nature of these experiences troubled her, and she shared her misgivings with members of her interdenominational prayer group. They felt that her ability was a gift from God and encouraged her to follow the gift wherever it might lead.

That gift led her in one instance to a Doberman that was being used as a guard dog at a large used-car lot. He had established a reputation in the neighborhood as a vicious beast. She passed this corner several times and on each occasion distinctly heard someone calling her name. It also seemed to her to be a call for help. She would look around, but only the dog would be in sight. She finally realized that it must be the Doberman who was calling out to her. She approached him, and he allowed her to pet him. She recalls the strange looks she received from passersby, for even while she stroked his head and back the dog snarled at people on the other side of the fence.

Loneliness had led him to call out to her, he said. He was desperate for loving attention and despised the image as a dangerous creature that resulted in his alienation from people.

Beatrice's gift led her to confide in a few friends, who confided in a few other friends, and the young woman soon found herself consulting on all kinds of pets. She went back to school to study anatomy, chemistry, zoology, and psychology. In the years since, she has communicated with many kinds of animals, from lizards to leopards.

Her experiences with animals opened the way for an

important contribution to the knowledge of humans. Like Patricia St. John, who works with dolphins as well as people, Lydecker is now communicating with nonverbal persons: the severely retarded, autistic children, stroke victims, and cerebral palsy sufferers.

Lydecker once worked with a two-year-old institutionalized child who had never acknowledged the existence of any other living being. Shut off from the world, he had responded to nothing that was done for him. But Beatrice communicated with him and found the child was suffering from severe emotional and physical trauma caused at birth. He wanted to return to the security and comfort of the womb, and the only thing he seemed to enjoy was being rocked.

Ms. Lydecker discovered—and later had the information confirmed by the doctors—that the infant had been born to a thirteen-year-old girl who did not want the baby and who had a difficult time delivering. The staff started rocking the baby, and before Miss Lydecker left the institute the child begun crawling toward a person who was coming to rock him.

"Everything alive communicates basically in the same manner," Beatrice told me. "It is subjective communication, which we all have as children, but as we grow up and start to use language we tend to lose this quality. Subjective communication allows you to say what you really feel."

Lydecker describes this type of communication as somewhat like a dream, "only the person is wide awake. Mental pictures come through in which one sees, hears, tastes, and experiences life.

"Any animal can read your mind," she states. "The thought is in the pictures, and this is what the pets see;

for this reason a person who thinks he may get bitten by a dog stands a pretty good chance of having his mental picture fulfilled. Pets also see images of owners even when those images are not directly related to the pet." She told how a German shepherd had taken up the habit of tearing up tissue. The shepherd's master had died, and the psychic learned that the dog was trying to share his mistress's grief. Distance, it seems, has little bearing on the communication between people and their pets. According to Lydecker, the animals will receive images from their owners who may be thousands of miles away, telling them, for example, when the owners are in danger or preparing to return home. For this reason, she says, pet owners who place their pets in kennels while they are on vacation and then worry about them the entire time shouldn't be surprised to return home and find that the pets have been ill or haven't been eating.

Lydecker, who is sometimes referred to as the touring animal analyst, travels the country in a van with three German shepherds and two cats. She has casual chats as well as deep conversations with animals. Her little thirteen-year-old male Pomeranian told her he had been lost in Las Vegas by his original owner—Julie or Judy, she isn't sure which—but that it was all right for her to keep the dog because he had not been with his previous owner long enough for her to be deeply attached to him.

Animals, like people, aren't always in a conversational mood. One day Lydecker's German shepherd, Princess, was staring wistfully out the window. Assuming that something important was on the dog's mind, she started to tune in, but in a few seconds

Princess looked toward her and distinctly told her to mind her own business. Roy Rogers' horse, Trigger, Jr., took one look at her and turned away!

But the calves at the rodeo told her they enjoyed the rough-and-tumble life of the rodeo, although they couldn't stand the fellow with the "hot stick"—evidently referring to the man with the electric prod used for prompting the calves to jump into the arena.

The great racing horse of a few years back, Secretariat, told Lydecker that he missed the company of his former groom, was lonely for the exciting activity of racing, and missed the sheer joy of running. He said he was bored with lazing around the pasture and being used as a stud. Lydecker explained that animals do not get much emotional thrill out of sex; for them, it's entirely physical.

Most pets are overfed and underexcited, much too pampered and often bored. "Owners are stubborn," Lydecker explained. "I've discovered that some pets can't stand their owners. In these situations I try to suggest tactfully to the owner that perhaps the pet needs a new home. I remember one session in which the owner kept repeating, 'But he's been with us for three years. The poor thing would never adjust to another home.' And all this time the dog was appealing to me, 'Get me away from these people.'"

Lydecker helps many owners find lost pets and has successfully located animals even long distances from their home. She tunes in and listens to the lost animal describe its surroundings, including houses, cars, and sometimes names. A fat scrapbook she keeps to document this work is filled with letters from pet owners expressing their gratitude, many of which state, "I still don't understand how you did it, but. . . ."

How can we understand the way Mojave Dan, Fred Kimball, and Beatrice Lydecker talk with animals? Is it really so strange, or is it that we have forgotten how to communicate directly with other life forms and imagine that verbal language is the only way? Isn't it possible that all life forms, large and small, have their being within a universal consciousness?

Interspecies communication is less difficult to accept if we entertain the possibility that all living things are thoughts within the mind of God, who has no difficulty whatsoever in understanding them. It follows, then, that the closer we come to the realization of our place within this omnipotence, the more we will understand the other inhabitants.

2

Talking with Plants

Most of us do not think of plants as fellow communicators; they play other roles in our lives. We appreciate a well-kept garden, the familiarity of an old shade tree, the succulence of home-grown vegetables. Receiving these gifts of nature, we have a greater or lesser gratitude to members of the plant kingdom for serving us aesthetically, nutritionally, and in many other ways.

Some rare souls, however, show a deeper appreciation. They caress, talk, sing, and meditate with plants. They express their thoughts and feelings while listening carefully and intensely to sense the plants' responses. They believe our world is to be shared, with each species bestowing its gifts on the others. They understand both plants and humans not as entities separate from this earth family but as beings endowed with qualities that can interact with other species. To these individuals, all forms of life are connected, expressions of the one universal consciousness.

Fred Kimball told us that if you want to know something about the horse, ask the horse. Others like George Washington Carver, Derald G. Langham, and Luther Burbank would have suggested that we direct our questions about the plant kingdom to one or more of its members. They did, and the answers they apparently received guided them to become legendary plant scientists who awed and confounded other scientists of their time.

Even as a small child George Washington Carver revealed an uncanny knowledge of all living things. The farmers in the small Missouri town of Diamond Grove noticed the fragile black boy wandering for hours over the land, examining various plants and bringing back varieties with which he healed sick animals. Entirely on his own, the boy established a garden in a remote piece of bottom land. Using salvage lumber and other materials he built a secluded greenhouse in the woods. Once asked what he was doing alone so many hours, Carver replied, "I go to my garden hospital and take care of hundreds of sick plants."

His special talent did not go unnoticed by farmers' wives, who brought him their sick house plants, asking him to make them bloom. Carver sang to the plants as he placed them gently in tin cans filled with soil of his own concoction. He covered them carefully at night and took them out to "play" in the sun during the day. Returning the thriving and blooming plants to their owners, he was often asked how he could work such miracles. Carver replied modestly: "All flowers talk to me, and so do hundreds of living things in the wood. I learn what I know by watching and loving everything."

Carver's parents were financially unable to provide him an education, but one day he ran across an old "blue speller." It opened up to him an entirely new world: the world of books. The boy devoured the spelling book, which constituted his only source of formal education until he was ten. At this age he learned of a school in a nearby town and asked permission to attend. At the school he supported himself by doing chores and other odd jobs, and he slept wherever he could find a place to lay his head. Within a year he had mastered all that the teacher in this country school could teach him. He hitchhiked to Fort Scott, Kansas, where for seven years he worked as a cook, dishwasher, laundryman, and housekeeper before he received the coveted high school diploma.

While studying at Simpson College in Indianola, Iowa, Carver lived in a woodshed and survived by taking in laundry. For his senior year, he transferred to Iowa State College at Ames, where he received his bachelor's degree in science. Then he went on to obtain his master's degree.

Because of his superior scholarship, Iowa State hired him for a faculty at Ames and soon put him in charge of the bacteriological laboratory, a greenhouse, and the department of systematic botany.

One day Dr. Booker T. Washington, the famous black educator, discovered Carver and asked him to come to Tuskegee Institute, a pioneering institution with little to offer in the way of salary or equipment. Carver would not reply until he had gone into the woods alone and talked it over with God. He returned with his answer.

Carver's arrival in Tuskegee was characteristic of his unique nature. When members of the welcoming committee went to the station to greet him, the train had already gone, and no one was in sight. Since they had not met him on the way, they wondered if he had missed his train—until one of them caught sight of a slim figure strolling up the track, hurrying first to one side, then to the other, as he discovered a flower or plant that was new to him.

At Tuskegee Institute Carver faced a task of heading up an agricultural department with no laboratory in which to teach. He started with a wooden bench containing apparatus that he pulled together himself. He made hub caps into crucibles and bottles into beakers. Other equipment came from various junk piles.

Having created a laboratory in which to teach his students, Carver made his next step to create a laboratory with which to teach the South.

The South had one big money crop: cotton. Even when the boll weevil and closing markets combined to make cotton inadequate to support the farmers, most of them still clung to it. Carter had not been in the South more than a few weeks when he discovered that the monotonous planting of a single crop was sucking the fertility from the soil. To counteract the despoliation by thousands of sharecroppers, he decided to set up an experimental station. He created a private laboratory, christened "God's Little Workshop," in which he sat for hours communing with plants.

For many years Carver worked experimentally to learn how to divert Alabama's addiction to cotton. His studies revealed that the peanut could survive in the depleted soil. His chemistry taught him that the peanut equaled beefsteak in protein and potatoes in carbohy-

drates.   Pondering one night what could be done with
the peanut, he stared at one of the plants and asked,
"Why did the Lord make you?"   Almost immediately he
received the answer: "You have three things to go by:
compatibility, temperature, and pressure."

Carver locked himself in his laboratory, and for a
sleepless week he worked to break down the peanut into
its chemical components and to expose than to various
conditions of temperature and pressure. He discovered
that a third of the nut was made up of seven different
oils. He analyzed and synthesized, took apart and
recombined, and by the end of that week he had developed twenty-four new products.

With his products in hand, Carver rallied farmers to
meetings in the hope of persuading them to abandon cotton in favor of peanuts, which he argued would be a far
more valuable cash crop. He asked that they rotate
peanuts with sweet potatoes, which he revealed also produced a cornucopia of products.

Because of the strangely unaccountable source from
which Carver's magic with plants sprang, his methods
remained totally bewildering to scientists. Visitors discovering Carver working at his bench amid a clutter of
plants, soils, molds, and insects were confused by the
simplicity of his replies to their persistent requests that he
reveal his secrets.

To one puzzled science reporter he explained: "The
secrets are in the plants. To elicit them you have to love
them enough."

"But why do so few people have your power?" the
man asked. "Who besides you can do these things?"

"Everyone can," Carver replied, "if only they believe it."

"I never grope for methods," he once said. "The method is revealed the moment I am inspired to create something new. I live in the woods. I gather specimens and listen to what God has to say to me. After my morning talk with God I go into my laboratory and begin to carry out His wishes for the day."

On another occasion he said: "When I touch that flower, I am not merely touching that flower. I am touching infinity. That little flower existed long before there were human beings on this earth. It will continue to exist for thousands, yes, millions of years to come. . . . How do I talk to a little flower? Through it I talk to the Infinite. And what is the Infinite? It is that silent, small force. It isn't the outer physical contact. No, it isn't that. The Infinite is not confined in the visible world. It is not in the earthquake, the wind or the fire. It is that still small voice that calls up the fairies. There are certain things, often very little things, like the little peanut, the little piece of clay, the little flower that cause you to look within—and then it is that you see into the soul of things."

Another plant specialist also went to the plants themselves for his answers. A man called by some "the father of modern agriculture in Venezuela" and by others "the father of genetic gardening," Dr. Derald G. Langham, a plant geneticist, was teaching genetics at the Universidad Central de Venezuela when World War II broke out. He returned to the United States to enlist in the army, but he was asked instead by the United States government to return to Venezuela and make the nation agriculturally self-sufficient in grain crops.

Langham faced the challenge by turning back to his experiences as a child growing up on an Iowa farm, when he had discovered that if he went into the woods, sat by a large tree, and allowed himself to become absolutely quiet, the animals of the forest would soon forget he was there. He could close his eyes and sense their energies without seeing them. In Venezuela, he tried to do the same kind of thing with the grains he was developing. He walked through the fields and said, "I need to know which ones of you have the power to resist drought, high winds, and excess rains." The approach worked, allowing him to supplement the standard tests and procedures for producing gene pools.

"I could communicate with the plants," Langham explained, "for I found that the energy field which enveloped the plants was similar to the one which enveloped myself. Through this connectedness I was able to understand their language."

Luther Burbank, another who communicated directly with plants, ushered in the new age of horticulture. While his dreams remained impossible ones for other plant scientists, his guidance came from watching, touching, and listening to the plants.

Even the non-editorializing *Encyclopedia Americana* asserted that the most important factor in Burbank's success was his innate sympathy with nature, assisted by the practical education in plant biology derived from fifty years of constant study and experiment, which helped him understand "correlations and outcomes of plant growth which seem to have been visible to no other man."

Burbank's vision, which established him with the press as the "Wizard of Horticulture," infuriated botanists who were unable to comprehend the Magic of his non-traditional methods. Equally in awe but fascinated by Burbank's discoveries was Hugo De Vries, an Amsterdam professor, later to be celebrated for carrying on Darwin's life work with his own theories of mutation, who was himself enough of a visionary to investigate what he considered to be incredible studies.

In 1892, De Vries happened upon a copy of Burbank's 52-page nurseryman's catalog, "New Creations in Fruits and Flowers." It had been published in Santa Rosa, California, and immediately created a sensation in the United States. While other catalogs of the times contained a few novelties, Burbank's offering contained not a single plant known to humans! The "Wizard" was offering a whole new world of plants, and the Dutch scientist had to see this for himself.

What De Vries discovered growing in Burbank's front yard at the end of his six-thousand-mile journey to visit Burbank was a fourteen-year-old Paradox walnut tree much larger than the Persian variety that was four times its age, along with a monkey-puzzle tree with twenty-pound nuts! De Vries was later to explain that he was dumbstruck to find that in Burbank's small home where he worked there was neither a laboratory nor a library. Burbank kept his work notes on scraps of paper torn from brown paper bags and on the backs of envelopes, De Vries discovered.

He was told by the plant breeder that the work was generally a "matter of concentration and the rapid elimination of nonessentials." As regards his laboratory, the plant breeder explain that he didn't need to keep notes because the plants told him what to do.

De Vries was not alone in his perplexity. Hundreds of American scientists visited the magical gardens at Santa

Rosa and, bewildered by Burbank's seeming lack of research, referred to him on occasion as a charlatan. Burbank did little to appease these criticisms in his evaluations of the botanical fraternity, telling the San Francisco Floral Congress in 1901 that:

"The chief work of the botanists of yesterday was the study and classification of dried, shriveled plant mummies whose souls had fled. They thought their classified species were more fixed and unchangeable than anything in heaven and earth than we can now imagine. We have learned that they are plastic in our hands as clay in the hands of the potter or color on the artists' canvas and can readily be molded into more beautiful forms and colors than any painter or sculptor can ever hope to bring forth."

But De Vries was not narrow-minded and accepted Burbank as a "natural-born genius" whose work "compels our highest admiration."

Burbank was an enigma, and he remains one to this day. He was born in a rural Massachusetts farm village in 1849. His early education consisted of reading the work of Henry Thoreau and other naturalists like Louis Agassiz and Alexander von Humboldt. He was also deeply impressed by Charles Darwin's *The Variation of Animals and Plants Under Domestication.*

What could have been easily overlooked by most gardeners did not escape notice by Burbank's attentive eyes. He spotted a seed ball in his potatoes. This vegetable very rarely sets seeds and is usually propagated by cutting the tubers into segments, with each piece containing one or more buds. Burbank knew that potato seeds would not grow tubers true to type, and that good or bad, large or small, the results would be mongrels. Yet this unknown offered the possibility of a miracle potato. This vision became a turning point in Burbank's young life, for one of the seed ball's twenty-three seeds yielded a plant whose offspring doubled the average yield. The potato was large, smooth, and an excellent baker, and its skin rather than being red was creamy-white.

A Massachusetts seedman, who claimed that it was the best potato he had ever eaten, paid Burbank $150 for it, naming it the "Burbank," and today it dominates the United States potato market.

Burbank's second step toward becoming a legend was taken in 1882 when he took on an assignment that other nurserymen in the area considered to be impossible. A new variety of plums known as prunes were becoming popular to California orchards as a money-making fruit. In March of that year a Petaluma banker asked Burbank if he could deliver twenty thousand young prune trees for a planting in December. He told Burbank that no one else was willing to accept the challenge, claiming that it would take two years to accomplish this feat.

It occurred to Burbank that almonds, also a member of the genus Prunus, would sprout much faster than the hard stones of plums, so he forced the oval-shaped nuts to sprout in warm water—a trick he had used on corn in Massachusetts. Yet, even with this gain, the seedlings were not ready for budding until June. Time was of the essence. Burbank obtained a cash advance from the banker and hired all available nursery help in the area. His crews worked around the clock. When they had finished, four months remained for Burbank's small seedlings to grow to approximately five feet in height and be ready for delivery. Apparently, his prayers were answered, for by Christmas he was able to deliver 19,500 trees to the grateful banker. Burbank's reputation had been established.

Burbank originated and introduced a remarkable series of plums and prunes. No fewer than fifty varieties were included in his list of offerings, and some of them, notably the Gold, Wickson, Apple, October, Chalco, America, Climax, Formosa, Bartlett, Santa Rosa, and Beauty plums, and the Splendor, Sugar, Giant, and Standard prunes, are among the best-known and most successful kinds now grown.

One of Burbank's most interesting experiments was the successful production of a whole new series of giant spineless cactus, both for forage and fruit—edible for humans and livestock. Burbank told Paramahansa Yogananda that during the year-long procedure of cross-breeding he first had to pull thousands of cactus thorns from his hands with pliers. "While I was conducting my experiments with cacti," he explained, "I often talked to the plants to create a vibration of love.

Burbank's power of love subtly nourished the plants, making everything grow better and bear fruit more abundantly, according to Manly Palmer Hall, founder and president of the Philosophical Research Society. "Burbank explained to me that in all his experimentation he took plants into his confidence, asked them to help, and assured them that he held their small lives in deepest regard and affection."

After a visit to Burbank, Helen Keller, deaf and blind, wrote in "Outlook for the Blind": "He has the rarest of gifts, the receptive spirit of a child. When plants talk to him, he listens. Only a wise child can understand the language of flowers and trees."

Burbank was quite sure about his relationship with plants. He did not question that he was in communication with them. He told Manly Hall that plants are intelligent and can communicate with human beings. "Obviously, they communicated with him," Hall states in the *The Inner Lives of Minerals, Plants and Animals*. "Most of his experiments depended upon mutual cooperation between Mr. Burbank and his plants. He secured this by getting down on his knees and explaining to the shrubs the entire purpose of the experiment."

Plants have more than twenty sensory perceptions but, because they are different from ours, we cannot recognize them, Burbank told Hall. "He was not sure," Hall noted, "that the shrubs and flowers understood his words, but he was convinced that by some telepathy, they could comprehend his meaning."

Burbank's belief in the personalization of his plants is illustrated by an article he wrote in 1906 for *Century* Magazine in 1906: "The most stubborn living thing in this world, the most difficult to swerve is a plant once fixed in certain habits. Remember that this plant has preserved its individuality all through the ages; perhaps it is one which can be traced backward through eons of time in the very rocks themselves. Do you suppose, after all these ages of repetition, the plant does not become possessed of a will, if you so choose to call it, of unparalleled tenacity?"

It is curious that when the great earthquake of 1906 devastated San Francisco and reduced Santa Rosa to rubble, not a pane of glass in Burbank's large greenhouse near the center of town was even cracked. Apparently, Burbank was less bewildered by this turn of events than his fellow townsmen, although he was careful not to mention it, but he surmised that his communing with the forces of nature and his success with plants had perhaps protected his greenhouse.

The perception of the connectedness of all life forms and man's relatedness to the plant kingdom, so obvious to George Washington Carver, Derald Langham, and Luther Burbank, never ceased to confuse more traditional members of the scientific community. Communication with the plants themselves just didn't fit into their restricted understanding of nature. Yet it was this vision of these rare plant geniuses that allowed them to change forever the face of agriculture.

3

Saint Francis, A Saint for All God's Children

❦

Although saints making friends with animals is one of the most tender chapters in the history of Christianity, it is not one that is well remembered. Sometimes it seems as though Saint Francis of Assisi is the only saint that people of all faiths recognize and accept. His statue stands in thousands of suburban gardens, where the owners tell stories of the way the saint cherished mice who tormented him in his cell and of the fish who, after he saved it from the cookpot, waited for Saint Francis at the shore and swam beside his boat. Part of the legend of the saint must be real. For Saint Francis, like his Master, so loved the world that the smallest inhabitant of it called upon his pity.

Saint Francis of Assisi continues to play an important role in the lives of many people. Only a person of his spiritual maturity could so completely love and communicate with all living creatures. Because all living things were an expression of God, to Saint Francis they were to be loved and cared for. And to this day people look to Saint Francis as not only a saint who communicated with animals but as the messenger demonstrating that this kind of love, embracing everyone and everything, is possible in the world.

Saint Francis has played an important role in my wife's and my life and that of a number of our friends. Our experiences at a special place in the Colorado Rockies, where we have returned each year for twenty-five years for spiritual retreats, may be useful to those who also have had, or would like to have, an experience with the dimension of Saint Francis that to us is very much alive today.

Nestled in a grove of large spruce trees in Deer Creek Canyon southwest of Denver is a garden of Saint Francis. It can be easily overlooked by motorists winding their way up the unpaved road to a growing number of building sites. The casual observer would most likely see only a lodge and possibly the partly-hidden chapel on a rise a short distance away.

But to those of us who go there each summer seeking solitude, meditation, and quiet unplanned discussions, the garden is important, it becomes the nucleus and perhaps the symbol of our sharing, and during our absence it remains large in our memories.

The property, sometimes called "The Restorium" and other times "Spruce Tree House," was established by a teacher who wrote under the name of Elizabeth Keyes and whose real name was Laurel Chivington. Although the site of workshops, ceremonies, weddings, christenings, lectures, and teaching, it also served over the years as a sanctuary to persons from many walks of life holding a variety of philosophies, all of them seeking, it would seem safe to venture, a greater clarity of vision.

It seemed to those of us who were Chivington's students that Saint Francis of Assisi was the saint in residence, for his presence was called into our awareness not by memorials or references to his life and contributions but by our sharing with the trees, the sky, the small creatures sometimes hovering or sometimes scurrying nearby, and with one another. We felt ourselves to be the saint's guests, and no host could have made us more welcome. This appeared to be equally true for the squirrels, chipmunks, larks, and hummingbirds, always there in abundance, but also the deer, stray dogs, and cats. Somehow, they knew this was a protected place.

Although legend had it that the location had once been an Indian healing place, the legend didn't account for what seemed like protection of the property by unseen hands. It was important to Laurel and those of us who spent time there that a spiritual environment be maintained, but once she rented a cabin to a couple who drank and argued. One night, following a loud verbal battle, all of the appliances in the cabin stopped working. An electrician could find nothing wrong, and several hours later the appliances were functioning again. A few days later, however, there was a repeat of the electrical anomaly. The arguers complained but stayed on—until the night of the mountain lion, which seemed to be summoned by a spiritual protector. While they were sitting at the kitchen table drinking and yelling at each other, a mountain lion landed with a terrifying scream on the roof above them. At the break of dawn they vacated the cabin.

On another occasion, a large motorcycle gang invaded Deer Creek Canyon and demonstrated little respect for the inhabitants' property. The numbers grew, and the invasion spread farther along the canyon—until it came within a mile of the Restorium, when the area was drenched by a local downpour. The road was so eroded that travel on it became impossible. Within two days all gang members had left the canyon. Spiritual intercession? We'll never know, but the canyon had never been so inundated by water, nor has it since.

Saint Francis treated all animals as equals, whether he was addressing a rabbit, cicada, turtledove, or donkey. If they were creatures of God, they were, by definition, his brothers and sisters. The flowers of the fields, the grass, the trees, earthworms—all were brothers and sisters. No stem could be cut off, no insect crushed without a warning from Saint Francis. At Deer Creek Canyon, sitting in the garden with my back against a tree watching a pair of ground squirrels chase each other around the shrine to Saint Francis that we constructed many years ago, I find it easy to believe anyone spending a week here would probably never intentionally hurt an animal again.

Some of the tales about Saint Francis may sound fictitious, such as the story of the grasshopper that on a winter midnight came to help him sing his office, leaving its tiny tracks in the snow to shame the monks who had been too lazy to assist. Or they may seem to be the result of coincidence, as in the story that on the evening of his death a cloud of larks, grieving for him, wheeled over his house and sang their farewells.

The larks, like the other animals of his time, were los-
ing a great friend. He felt so strongly for the mistreated
animals of his day, for the whipped horses, captured
birds, and hungry dogs, that he went to the burghers, to
the governors, and finally to the emperor, pleading for a
law protecting them from abuse. He asked that farmers
be forced to treat their cattle kindly. He wanted towns
and corporations to take time off from levying taxes to
scatter crumbs on the frozen roads. He asked for hostels
where strays could be housed and fed, and he raged
against the caging of larks. His requests for the most part
went unanswered, but in Assisi to this day, at the time of
the Angelus, people feed his birds in the market place.

Although the best-known saint who cared for animals, Francis was not the only one. Gerasimus the Abbot
bound up the wounds of a lion he found limping along
the river Jordan with a thorn in his paw. Walaricus fed
the birds that came to eat while he admonished intruding
visitors, "Do let these innocents eat in peace."

Regardless of how needy they were themselves,
saints always cared for the poor, human and otherwise.
Aldemar, for instance, permitted bees to make a hive in
one of his cupboards. And Martin de Porres, a sort of
Peruvian St. Francis, reportedly treasured even the ver-
min that chewed on the monastery vestments. He
excused the destructive behavior of mice and rats on the
grounds that "the poor little things were insufficiently
fed." Martin was a one-man Humane Society and kept a
hospital for dogs and cats at his sister's house. One can
guess that she, too, was somewhat of a saint.

It is recorded that kind old William Firmatus, a

French anchorite who lived in the eleventh century, had so much power over animals that the peasants would plead with him to ask the rabbits and goats to stop despoiling their fields. And he did. With these animals all about him, the goats searching his pockets for food and the birds nestled in his habit, he asked them to eat more sparingly in the gardens and fields. Apparently, his requests worked most of the time, but if gentleness didn't work, he would take severer measures. Once the countryside was being ravaged by a wild boar—a situation not uncommon in the Brittany of 1090. He found the boar, took it by one ear, led it to a cell, shut it up, and told it to fast all night. When he set it free the next morning, it was cured of its marauding tendencies, so the story goes.

But the protection didn't always travel from saint to beast; sometimes it was the other way around. A huge gray mongrel made himself the bodyguard for Don John Bosco when that dynamic defender of delinquent boys was endeavoring to establish the Salesian Order. No one seemed to know where Grigio came from, just as they didn't know the origin of the homeless children Don John gathered about him. Grigio simply turned up one day when the saint needed him and fought off a mugger, who apparently didn't know how destitute Don John kept himself for the sake of his children. From that time on the dog remained on hand to defend the saint against danger. Grigio intercepted foes, warned Don John once of an ambush, and proved more reliable than the Italian police. But after the saint persuaded the government that he could be trusted to run the home for the boys, his projects thriving and the Salesian Order safe, the dog appeared only once more—for dinner at the refectory. He rubbed his head against the saint's habit, offered his paw, and then wandered out of sight, never to be seen again.

These stories, like music, linger on in the mind, for most of us would like to remember the communicating that exists between humans and other beings. Perhaps the tales aren't so mysterious when we remind ourselves that many of the old friars lived quiet lives, having learned to move softly in their wilderness. Is it so strange that the rabbits and deer, even the bears and wolves, could become their companions? What is so marvelous about Finbarr? He merely milked a doe when cow's milk was in short supply. And it's not so difficult to believe that Theon of Thebaud walked in the desert at night with "the wild things of the desert walking by his side."

Saint Francis of Assisi was not a lover of nature in the sense that this is usually understood. The phrase generally implies the acceptance of the material world as a pleasant sort of place. During the romantic period of literature, it was common to imagine a hermit finding reclusion in the ruins of a chapel and seeking peace in the harmony of solemn forests and silent stars while he mused over the meaning of life. Within this context, nature might be loved as a background. But for Saint Francis nothing was ever in the background. Everything emerged with a distinct character and existence of its own. It was alive, functioning with a vitality and destiny of its own. He experienced all of life as dramatic, distinct from its setting, not all of a piece like a picture but in action, like a play. Life was not something to be observed but something to experience. Saint Francis wanted to bond and communicate with every life form in it.

Sometimes we say that a certain man can't see the

wood for the trees, but Saint Francis did not want to see the wood for the trees. He wanted to see each tree—flower, bird, rabbit, human—as a separate and sacred thing, a child of God. This is the quality in which, as a poet, he was the opposite of the sentimental pantheist. Saint Francis did not call nature his mother; he called a rabbit or a squirrel (not all rabbits and squirrels) brother or sister. To him they were individual creations, beings assigned by their creator to particular places and roles, with whom he could communicate and share life.

At one point in his life Saint Francis struggled to decide whether to live a secluded life of prayer or to carry on his mission with others; after deciding that he must live the life of service, he went on the road in pursuit of those who would listen to him. As he walked he grew aware of the oneness pervading all things, and a sensation of overpowering love overcame him. He felt close to earth and cloud, leaf and blade of grass, everything under the sun. As he walked, the birds seemed to sense the delight in his soul. They flew up from the ground and down from the trees, surrounding him in song. When he stood in their midst, they gathered around him in a circle, filling the road, the bushes, and the trees as though seeking audience in a great concert hall. The saint raised his hand, for he understood that he was being asked to preach to his feathered brothers and sisters. He advised them to praise God for the benefits bestowed upon them and to avoid ingratitude. The birds then opened their beaks, beat their wings, and bowed their small heads reverently as they sang. Saint Francis raised his arms and sang with them. Then he blessed them—his brothers and sisters—and the flock flew up and dispersed in the air. One of Saint Francis's biographers asserts that the power of Saint Francis's speech on that particular day went beyond that of human understanding of language and established communication at a universal level. As such, it was understood by humans and the animal kingdom alike.

Shortly after his sermon, Saint Francis arrived at the little town of Alviano, preparing to preach to the townspeople, who had come to listen to his words. It was toward nightfall, a time when hundreds of swallows circled over the square, which resounded with their unceasing twitter. As the crowd waited in tense silence for the sermon to begin, the swallows kept coming in even greater numbers, circling closer and closer and filling the square with their voices so that nothing else could be heard.

The saint waited for a while, watching the swallows. Finally he turned to them and said in his soft voice: "My brothers and sisters, the swallows, it is now time for me to speak. You have been speaking enough all the time." And immediately the swallows were silent. They settled down on the cornices and roofs of the buildings, lowered their heads in worshipful respect, and listened silently to the sermon, as did the people below in the square. When Saint Francis had finished and the people sang a song of jubilation and praise, the swallows too joined in with voices of joy. The acceptance of its reality established the success of the communication.

The inhabitants of Alviano, witnessing this extraordinary occurrence, exclaimed: "A miracle! A miracle! A saint!"

The bells in the church tower began ringing. Who had set them going? The entire population of Alviano was in the market place. No one had left. And while the bells were ringing—the bells that no one had set ringing—the voices of people and swallows merged in one great song of jubilation and praise. People came and asked Saint Francis to admit them to the ranks of his disciples. They were willing to abandon their castles or their homes and friends to follow him in poverty, humility, and love.

Saint Francis's miracle of the birds marks the beginning of a new epoch in the cultural history of the West. Through it the word of God broke the isolation of the human world and penetrated the world of nature. And through it, art and poetry and finally science achieved a similar breaking down of the isolation and restriction of human emotions and thoughts. The medieval rigidity with which Byzantine painting represented its saint disappeared entirely, and the more natural representation of the living and moving human figure as well as the portrayal of nature in art had their beginnings in the artistic portrayal and representation of the legend of the birds. Interspecies communication had become a communion.

Before the time of Saint Francis, medieval piety had lost itself in supersensual speculations, coming dangerously close to paralysis through theological sophistry. With Saint Francis the windows of nature opened and the view was cleared for the veneration of God in the veneration of nature. And just as the artist could look at nature and derive inspiration from it with a clear conscience and without harming his or her faith, so the medieval people of learning could indulge their craving for knowledge and look into nature to investigate its laws.

This decisive turn in the history of Western thought

led to a reconciliation of the spirit of Christianity with love of nature, two views that long had been incompatible with each other. It was a reconciliation made possible through Saint Francis's loving imitation of Christ. His sermon to the birds was the first blessing given to the union, which led to the birth of a new Christian faith enriched by new beauty and knowledge of nature. The original joy and beauty of the Christian way of life, which had been forgotten for more than a thousand years, came to the fore again through Saint Francis's example and message.

The saint lived his love for all of God's creatures. Once as he returned from a begging tour heavily laden with all sorts of gifts and food, he came upon a woodcutter chopping down a tree. "Brother, do not chop off the whole tree, give it a chance to grow up again," said Saint Francis, and he offered the man his food by way of recompense. He always insisted that Brother Gardener reserve in his vegetable garden a place for flowers so that their beauty might bear witness to the splendors of God.

On another occasion, he saw a rabbit that was caught in a snare, and just as if it were a human being whom he had to free from a trap, he dropped everything and hastened to assist Brother Hare. And one early spring following an extremely dry year, the honey bees were having a difficult time; their food was almost gone. Saint Francis went out begging for honey and sweet wine and placed the gifts he received in a hollow tree, where his "sisters the bees" would find them. At Siena he helped the turtledoves build their nests and made sure every day that their young ones had enough to eat. Whenever he ate, he always left some of the food for the birds and animals.

Once when he and several of his brothers were eat-

ing their Christmas dinner by the roadside, a flock of
crows settled down in a clump of trees nearby. "Our
black sisters want to share our meal," stated Saint
Francis. "Quick, Leo, wait on them." Leo brought a loaf
of bread and trampled down the snow to prepare a table
for the birds while Saint Francis busied himself by breaking up the bread. The crows came flying down to get the
food; sparrows and hundreds of other birds joined them.
Meanwhile, Saint Francis looked on with joy at the feast.
"If I ever went to see the emperor," he said, "I would ask
him to issue a decree that everyone should broadcast at
Christmas time a certain quantity of grain all over the
countryside as a gift for the birds."

Once he met a farmer who was taking two sheep to
market to have them butchered. In order to save their
lives, he gave the farmer his coat in trade for the sheep.
He took them along and decided to be their guardian.
Another time while walking toward a town where he
planned to preach, he saw an ugly caterpillar. He picked
it up so that it wouldn't be stepped on and, putting it in a
clump of grass, spoke to it: "Some time you will be a
beautiful butterfly, Sister Caterpillar, just as our ugly and
sinful body will at one time release the soul which will
fly up to heaven in lightness and beauty."

Just as men and women of all classes were attracted
by the power of his love and left their established lives to
follow him, so did the animals succumb to the spell of
his universal brotherhood. Near Siena a whole flock of
sheep left their pasture and followed Saint Francis. In
Assisi a small lamb went with him wherever he was
going, accompanying him to the chapel and listening
with the other brothers to the mass. A pheasant that had

been presented to Saint Francis returned to him of its own free will when he turned it loose. In an olive tree not far from the cell where he lived for a time in solitude lived a cicada. "Come, sister Cicada," the saint said, "and praise the lord our Creator with a joyful song." And whenever he called, the cicada came, sat on his hand, and joined him softly in his songs of praise.

The inspiration of Saint Francis's words and personality not only fired the imagination of poets and artists, its irresistible force influenced great masses of ordinary men and women. It changed their habits of thought, their emotions and behavior, so fundamentally that far-reaching transformation of the social structure of the Middle Ages resulted from it.

It was his natural spontaneity, his love, and his total involvement with all forms of God's expressions that assured Saint Francis his following. He was not a pantheist in whose thoughts all of creation merged with his own self. Such philosophies would not have been understood by the common folk. But that a lover of life, one of such great and unselfish passion, would speak to a flower, a bird, a rabbit, a tree, as though they were his brothers and sisters, that he did not conceive of his ultimate identity with the abstract ideas of flowers and animals but was moved by a warm sensation of brotherly love for one specific buttercup or one lark—this genuineness was universally understood.

The interspecies communication between Saint Francis and the creatures of the earth thus contributed not only to a greater acceptance of all life forms but also to a deeper understanding of the role of humans in nature.

When Saint Francis quieted the swallows in the mar-

ket place of Alviano, he was no magician whose words
wove a spell of power over the creatures. A magician
might have elicited awe but could not have touched the
hearts of those who heard him, and he could not have
induced the inhabitants of a whole village to follow him.
This transformation could have been produced only by
one whose love of them—and whose overpowering love
of all creatures and of life itself—made him speak as
Brother Man to Sister Swallow. His simple and natural
intimacy with all of God's creatures stirred the people of
Alviano and gave them the assurance that this man was
sent by God and had received his power from God.

Perhaps the birds and the small creatures in the
woods have never been so much noticed and understood
as they were by Saint Francis. Yet his legacy lives on in
the hearts and minds of those individuals and groups
who struggle to protect the wildlife and the environment,
sometimes at considerable sacrifice. Perhaps some part
of him is there cheering them on in the rain forests, the
wildlife swamps, and the seas. Nor is it difficult to
believe that his spirit is there in those who reach out to
our little brothers and sisters with the firm belief that
interspecies communications is not at all an impossible
dream, that the vision demands fulfillment if the human
species is to be rescued from genocidal isolation.

4

Mother Wind, Brother Wolf

Native Americans who have remained close to their traditions demonstrate an atunement to the earth and its inhabitants that we have either forgotten or never achieved. Interspecies communication is to them not a subject to be studied, it is an essential component of their way of life. The earth—its prairies, forests, and mountains—is the Native Americans' cathedral and school. They listen, and they read it well.

This ability of Native Americans was revealed to some of us a number of years ago on the edge of the prairie called Flint Hills. We were participants in a conference sponsored by the Menninger Foundation on the Voluntary Control of Internal States. During the week-long gathering of ninety persons we were exposed to the scheduled teachings of Rolling Thunder, medicine man of the Shoshone nation, and several of us spent as much unscheduled time as we could find with him. He talked a great deal about the importance of interspecies communication and how we stood to gain from interacting with other intelligences than just the human one. Our discussions and his demonstrations centered mostly on creatures indigenous to the area. But on the final morning of the conference we discovered that his communication with all life expressions included the wind.

Rolling Thunder offered to provide us with an Indian sunrise service. The medicine man had told us to come to the edge of this hill and that he would join us. We gathered on the ridge of the hill overlooking the lake at Council Grove, Kansas. The cool early April breeze blowing across the lake in the pre-dawn hours encouraged those present to huddle close together.

A short time after we had gathered, Rolling Thunder came out of the shadows of the woods carrying a bundle of dried branches on his shoulders. Without a word to the group, he placed the wood on the ground a few feet from us and prepared it as a campfire. At the first touch of sun on the horizon, he started the ritual. But at the appropriate time to light the fire, the wind was blowing too strong for him to get it started.

Rolling Thunder stood and silently faced the south wind. He stood there for a few moments, and then he raised his right hand and held it up facing the wind. The wind stopped. Rolling Thunder knelt down and lighted the fire. As the flames leaped up through the branches, the medicine man stood. He faced south, nodded slightly and a strong southerly wind once again raced across the ridge. Without a word of explanation, Rolling Thunder turned toward the eastern sky and resumed the sunrise service.

I can still see us standing there in the growing light, the trees along the edge of the lake silhouetted against the rose dawn, glancing at one another furtively as if unsure what we were seeing. Here and there whispers intruded the silence briefly. We were all probably struggling with the meaning of what we had experienced. But what could we say, what questions could we ask of one another?

When the sunrise ritual had ended and we were making our way back toward the lodge for breakfast, each walked alone, unready to attach words to a happening not lending itself to language.

This was not our first experience of Rolling Thunder's relationship to the elements. Two days earlier at the conference, the Shoshone medicine man had performed a healing. One of the young scientists had arrived at the camp with a leg seriously injured during a soccer game. The conference was important to him, and he decided to attend in spite of his injury. But the leg had become infected, and during the day he withdrew to his bed with a fever. Late that afternoon he asked Rolling Thunder if he would perform a healing.

That evening the group gathered in the small auditorium. The injured man sat slumped in a chair at the front of the room as the medicine man prepared for the healing ceremony. Rolling Thunder lit a pipe and drew on it four times, once each while facing East, North, South, and West. As he did so, he uttered these words:

"To the East where the Sun rises.
To the North where the cold comes from.
To the South where the light comes from.

To the West where the Sun sets.
To the Father Sun.
To the Mother Earth."

He then handed the pipe to his patient, who also drew on it four times. The medicine man spoke to the young man about the injury and asked him why he wished to be healed. Once he was satisfied with the patient's answers, he faced the man and performed a high, wailing chant that went on for several minutes. At first, the chant came unmistakenly from the medicine man, but then it seemed to fill the room without originating at any single place.

The chant ended suddenly. Rolling Thunder had his patient lie down. After a few moments he placed his mouth on the wound, making a sucking sound. He did this several times, and after each session he spit what he had drawn from the wound into a bowl where he had earlier placed a piece of raw meat. When he was through with drawing infection from the wound, he spit into his hands, rubbed the hands together and placed them on the wound. He placed the patient in a chair and, taking a feather, made a number of sweeping motions around the young man's body. Now and then he would turn toward the bowl and shake the feather at it. The healing ceremony completed, Rolling Thunder left the room, ordering, as he did so, that the contents of the bowl were to be burned to ashes.

Several physicians examined the patient immediately. Their consensus was that the color of the leg had returned to normal, the swelling had decreased, and the flesh around the wound was flexible instead of hard.

The patient reported that he was no longer in pain. We had all witnessed the medicine man's ability to communicate with something other than humans.

During the five days of the conference Rolling Thunder talked to the group about Native American traditions, the training and discipline involved in being a medicine man or woman, the use of herbs, and the importance of communicating with plants to be used for nourishment and medicine. He explained that medicine men and women received power from certain animals and reptiles by taking those animals' lives with their bare hands and thus taking the animals' power—even the poison of the rattlesnake—within themselves and then never taking the lives of those creatures again. When it is necessary to kill an animal for food or clothing, he explained, it is imperative that apologies be made to the animal. Then every part of the animal must be put to good use.

"I'll tell you a few things that you can take with you," he said to us. "You can start with this. You can take a glass of water and pray over it and make medicine out of it. A lot of times the Indians will be caught with no medicine, and they want to cure a fever or some other illness. They'll take a glass of water, pray over it in the morning when the sun's coming up. When the sun's rising in the morning, vibration—what you call vibrations in the earth, we call it the Great Spirit's power—are strongest then, and they're bringing forth new life. When the sun starts to rise we make our prayer, and when you see the bottom of the sun, that's when it ends. Let the rays of the sun hit that water and you can make medicine out of it if that is what you need to do."

During the annual meeting of that same conference several years later, Mad Bear, medicine man of the Iroquois Indian Nation, taught us a valuable lesson about prayer. We had been meeting for two days, some fascinating presentations had been made by well-credentialed persons, and the participants were caught up in the euphoria of the mental stimulation. But by the morning of the third day, apparently, Mad Bear had had enough.

"I am impressed by your intelligence and the research you obviously have spent many years developing," Mad Bear stated to the group before the morning proceedings started. "Yet I am saddened," he continued, "that we have become so caught up, so hypnotized by our own importance that we have failed to express our gratitude to that life which made all of this possible . . . the food which has been prepared for us, the plants and animals who offered their lives to us so that we could live, the air we breathe, the grass that cushions our footsteps, the birds who give us song, the trees that shade us, the Great Spirit who created us. . . . " He paused to study the silent faces. "Are we humans so profound that we have nothing to gain from communicating with other inhabitants of this planet? And is it asking too much for us to take a few minutes to pray to the Great Spirit and for us to offer gratitude each morning before we get into other things?" Ashamed by our insensitivity and distorted priorities, we awkwardly shook our heads and mumbled our agreements. Prayer was not forgotten the remainder of that week, nor has it been overlooked during the conference in the years since.

The Council Grove conferences were not my first encounters with exceptional Native Americans. Where I was raised in southern Kansas many Cherokee and Chilloco Indians were our friends and neighbors. They farmed and ranched alongside us, and there had of course, been a lot of mixing of blood lines. As children we were aware of many of the Native American customs and beliefs. More than a few had been integrated into our own outlooks on life. Yet, looking back, what I feel was of even greater importance was the respect the Native Americans taught us for other creatures, for they communicated with their dogs, their horses, with everything in their environment. We were exposed to this interaction, and at least some of us never forgot.

Just as with any other race, there were Native Americans who were considered skilled and trained in the ways of nature. But I don't believe I understood the depth of the Indian experience until I became friends with a young Sioux girl, Lois Flying Cloud, during a summer in South Dakota.

During summer vacation while we were in college, two friends and I had followed the wheat harvest from Oklahoma to Canada. Rain held us up for a time in Winner, South Dakota. We made a few friends, and one of them introduced me to Lois Flying Cloud. It was during a church picnic in a park, and because it was a hot, lazy day it was easier to lie in the shade and talk than get involved with other activities. If my memory serves me correctly, it was some comment that Lois made about the tree shading us that intrigued me. The afternoon wore on, the shadows deepened, other members of our group became restless and wandered off, but I hardly noticed, for I was experiencing a shift in consciousness. The young Indian girl was moving my horizons. She

was acquainting me with an earth, a sky, the wind, the
creatures that moved and the beings who, rooted to the
ground, waited, with a pulse and an awareness. What
mesmerized me was her understanding of these life
forms not as an observer but as a participant. This was
to be the first of a number of magical days spent with
Lois Flying Cloud as my mentor.

Sometimes I would see her in the evening after coming in from the fields. She served as secretary for one of
the churches and was saving her money to study art. Since
she frequently worked in the evenings, I would sit in her
office and read until she finished, and we would go some
place to talk. But Sunday was our day together: a picnic
lunch, a hike into the hills, and the magic of discovery.

Lois was fortunate. She had been raised in an Indian
family whose members understood the need to cope with
the whites' culture. Yet they valued highly the mystical
insights of their people. These they passed along to their
children, and Lois Flying Cloud was a mystic.

"Listen carefully to the wind," she would tell me, "for
it brushes the soul of all living things. Some small particle
of everything it touches is borne with it on its travels.
Scents, pollen, dust, yes, but much more than these, for
there are whispers of sound that change ever so faintly by
the arrangement of that which is passed by the wind."

She would have me close my eyes and, taking my
hand, lead me to various places; I was to tell by the
sound of the wind what surrounded us: trees, rocks, hills,
grass. I would sit with eyes closed and point in her direction as she moved in a circle about me some hundred
feet away. Occasionally, I guessed her position correctly,
and when she rejoined me we would laugh about the

problems of getting a white man "in tune." When our roles were reversed and I led her about, she seemed to be more aware with eyes closed than I with mine open. "There is a large bird passing overhead," she said. I looked up to see a hawk gliding in the sky about us.

Later, lying on the grass, gazing lazily into the sky, I asked her, "How did you know the bird was there, Lois? You couldn't have heard it."

She didn't answer for a while. She rolled over and gazed into the grass as though watching some occurrence. Then slowly, "As me, Lois, I could not see or hear the hawk, something apart and not of me. But, then, I release myself and I am no longer locked in this body. I reach out and all that was not me becomes me . . . words are difficult. . . ." She ran her fingers through the grass, caressing it as though it were the hair of a loved one.

"When my spirit rides the wind, becoming one with all that is, I am no longer a girl seeing a hawk. I am just as much a hawk seeing a girl. Where do I end and the flying bird begin? I do not know. . . . I know only that he is part of my existence. He is there. I experience him within myself. Perhaps you would say that the hawk and I communicate telepathically. This may be, but I speak to the hill and the grass, and the hawk knows these, too, and we are all one, breathing and being breathed by the Great Wind."

Lois taught me that Indians move as best they can in conscious rhythm with what they call the Great Spirit, the unified Consciousness of all that is. All life forms are to be respected and loved as part of oneself, and this is not done only in the philosophical sense of sharing life upon this planet but in the belief that in an ultimate sense there is no separation.

On one of our Sunday outings, Lois reached out her
hand, and a red squirrel took a piece of bread from her
fingers. It did not scamper away. It sat on its haunches
close to her and nibbled away at the food. We had eaten
our lunch that day in a cottonwood grove bordering the
edge of a small meadow creek. I had noticed an odd-
looking bush some distance away and had gone to
inspect it. As I returned I saw Lois feeding the squirrel
and waited until the small creature despaired of begging
any more food and departed before I approached.

"You've made a friend," I said.

"Oh, yes, but he gave me more than he took."

"Do you mean friendship?"

"That, too, yes, but he offered me food in return." She
read the puzzled look on my face and added, "Before he
came to me for the bread he nibbled on the leaves of that
plant. It is a type of nettle, and he was telling me that it
could provide me food."

I thought about this for a moment and asked, "Have
you ever tasted a plant offered by an animal?"

There was no hesitation. "Oh, yes, often. They
wouldn't tell me this if it weren't so. Indians have
learned of most of their foods from the animals."

She talked of the beauty and the wisdom of the squirrel, the moth, the raven—all the creatures with whom we
share the earth. She spoke of them as expressions of the
Great Spirit. "What we really see as marvelous is the
Universal Being expressing a fox or expressing a lynx. . .
." Lois Flying Cloud ran a hand through her long black
hair; it caught a ray of sunlight racing through the leaves
and sparkled like a black diamond, framing a classic
young face cast in half-shadow. Lois was struggling with

an inheritance that demanded sharing.

"We become enchanted with the form of the horse or the owl," she said, "and imagine that they are limited in their intelligence and being and forget that they are expressions of the All-Knowing. Would we limit it? If this small creature is the Great Spirit expressing Himself, why do we not listen? Why do we imagine that God would create all manner of living things out of the substance of His being and yet limit Himself to existing only within the human? How could He manage that? How could the All-Knowing care for the hawk when He created him and care for him soaring in the sky, but not care when his body lies no longer moving on the ground? Why would He do that?"

I sat on the grass beside her and was staring away to the hills, listening, probing. "There are many mysteries that we do not understand," I offered.

"Mysteries, yes, there will always be these, Bill, but would there be fewer if we were to find that all of these creatures exist within and not outside of us?"

A silence fell between us, not as a break but as a bond, and it stated more than words. We remained until the first fireflies signaled the passing of the day. Hand in hand we made our way from the cottonwood grove, across the meadow, past the buffalo wallows, and up the cattle trail to town.

"I'll bet if they put their minds to it some of our four-footed friends could come up with some tests to prove they are more intelligent than we are," Lois said as we reached the last stretch of our journey. She giggled, and then we laughed, and it was almost all right that our day was ending.

The central message of the Indian medicine man or woman is that human nature is identical with the nature of the universe and that we can learn about our own nature from nature itself. Rolling Thunder points out that "The technological and materialistic path of contemporary Western society is the most unnatural way of life man has ever tried. The people of this society are farthest removed from the trees, the birds, the insects, the animals, the growing plants, and the weather. They are therefore the least in touch with their own inner nature. Unnatural things are so commonplace to the modern mind, it is little wonder natural things seem strange and difficult to face."

Doug Boyd, who studied and lived with Rolling Thunder in Nevada for a year before writing a book about him, told me that he was continually impressed by the medicine man's communication with plants, animals, and even the weather. On one occasion he and the medicine man were looking for herbs to make medicine. A strong thunderstorm came up, and they were being drenched. "Let's head for my shrine," Rolling Thunder said. "It won't be raining there." Boyd said that he imagined some structure in which they could hide from the weather. Instead, it was simply a circular stack of stones. But in a circle several feet around the shrine no rain was falling, even though heavy rain continued to pour down beyond that point.

On another occasion while looking for herbs, Boyd glanced up to discover Rolling Thunder wiggling his fingers above the leaves of some plants. Then he saw that the plant was covered by ants. The medicine man continued the wiggling of the fingers in a sort of herding fashion, and the ants scurried away. He did this time and again, and each time that he waved over a leaf the ants would depart quickly. "I saw him point his finger down a stem and move a column of ants as though his finger were a magnet and the ants little particles of iron," Boyd said.

On this same outing Boyd suddenly found himself in the company of a large rattlesnake. The snake was close to him, and his initial experience of fear gave way to an odd sense of elation as he remembered his mentor's respect for snakes. "Look at this!" he called to the group with him.

"Everyone turned," he states in his book. "Even the women were calm. Rolling Thunder knelt down close to the head of the snake and held out his hand. The snake coiled and raised its head to meet the hand. His hand and the snake's eyes were only inches apart. They both began to move. When the hand moved forward, the head went back. When the hand withdrew, the head followed. Rolling Thunder bobbed his head and the rattles buzzed. Now he extended both his hands and the snake swayed slowly between them, first to one side, then to the other. Rolling Thunder and the snake were eye to eye, and I watched, suspended. It was a dance. Rolling Thunder stopped and the snake became still, absolutely motionless. 'Now,' he said, 'watch him go on about his business.' He wheeled around on one foot and stood up with his back to the snake. The snake went limp, uncoiled, slid through a drain pipe under the highway, and was gone. No one said a word."

Rattlesnakes seem to feel a kinship for Indians. J. Allen Boone, who has studied the matter, believes that

while rattlesnakes seem to go out of their way to strike a
white man, they very seldom harm an Indian.

"Almost everywhere I went," Boone recounts in his
book, *Kinship with All Life*, "there was vicious and relent-
less warfare going on between white men and rattlesnakes; it was warfare to the death of either the man
or the snake. But I could find no such warfare between
Indians and the rattlesnakes. There seemed to be a kind
of gentlemen's agreement between them. In all my jour-
neying in deserts, prairies and mountains I never once
saw a rattlesnake coil, either by way of defense or attack
when an Indian walked into its close vicinity."

Boone speculates that whites have been taught to
despise the snake and to find it loathsome, to kill it. The
snake, he believes, picks up on this mental poison and
immediately goes on the defensive. Survival is at stake,
and the snake prepares for it. Indians, on the other
hand, Boone points out, transmit no hostility toward the
snake. When a snake and an Indian encounter one
another, they contemplate each other for a few moments
and then go on their respective ways. This might happen
because Indians, Boone asserts, move "in conscious
rhythm" with what is reverently called "the Big Holy,"
the great primary principle of all life, which creates and
animates all things and speaks with wisdom through
each of them. Boon believes that because of this universally operating law, an Indian operated "in silent and
friendly communion" with a rattler as "a much-admired
and much-loved 'younger brother' who was entitled to as
much life, liberty, happiness, respect and consideration
as he hoped to enjoy himself."

I was to witness this communication between

humans and other creatures when Doug Boyd invited me, along with about ten other white men and women, to meet with a council of Native American medicine men and women in a wooded campsite near Kansas City. The main reason for the gathering was to bring together medicine persons from the many Indian nations in order to learn whether they could agree on which of their traditions and beliefs could be shared with whites. If agreement could be reached, then they would meet with our group to share ideas about ways this communication could be accomplished. For two days we waited for the Indians' agreement in our separate camp some distance away in the woods. A messenger finally brought word that the Indians would meet with us the following morning. We spent a large part of that night trying to think what we had to offer the Native Americans in return.

When morning arrived, we formed a large circle and sat quietly in meditation while we awaited their arrival. When they came, most of them chanting and in their native dress, winding their way in a line through the trees, we opened our circle. They moved inside, formed their own circle, and sat cross-legged on the ground. It was an experience I shall never forget.

Many of the medicine men and women spoke of their beliefs, their prophecies, and their traditions. They also spoke of their fears about the problems we face in this country, of the things no longer held sacred, and of the damage being done to the earth. They felt that the time had arrived for Native Americans to speak up, not just in criticism but to also offer their knowledge in the search for solutions. We in turn did our best to let these sensitive and insightful persons know that we would serve as bridges between traditions.

Several hours later we celebrated what everyone felt was a successful council by eating together. This gave us the opportunity to become better acquainted. Although I didn't particularly seek him out, I found myself spending most of that afternoon with Bobby Woods, keeper of the sacred pipe for the Sioux of Ontario. I had the rare opportunity of walking in the forest with this medicine man and, for the most part, simply listening while he talked.

What I remember most about this encounter was not the dialogue between us, however fascinating, but the moments when he would spot a squirrel, for example, and then predict for me its movements across a space, up a particular tree, out a certain branch, then along another branch—even the pauses and waiting of the small creature. Remember, all of these descriptions preceded the squirrel's activities. He gave me this same kind of projected road map for a couple of ground squirrels and a rabbit. He would pause in our discussions to offer these animal game plans and then would immediately continue our conversations as though nothing had happened.

"See that hawk flying overhead?" Bobby Woods asked during one of our exposures to the open sky. "He is not hunting, he is scouting us and the other strangers in his territory. In a moment he will perch atop that third maple tree in that cluster of oaks." The hawk did exactly that, and before the large bird left the perch, Bobby Woods announced, "he will leave that tree and come to the locust by us. He will pause for a minute or so, and he will then fly to the roof of that church." He referred to a chapel in the woods built by the church that owned the property. The hawk followed this agenda as though it and the medicine man had agreed on a course of activity.

When I jokingly accused Bobby Woods of controlling his small brothers and sisters, he laughed and said, "No, I don't interfere with their lives, but because we are all part of the Great Spirit, we can share our thoughts and designs. If I experience them as being separate from myself, then I cannot know what they will do. But becoming one with them, I can know."

Late that afternoon both groups met with high-level authorities of the world's major religions. It was an historic gathering, one that anyone would be proud to be part of. Yet, during the meeting, my thoughts often drifted instead to Bobby Wood, profound philosopher and hilarious storyteller, who communicated with small scurrying creatures and dignified hawks.

Now I sit on the weathered stump of a once-large cottonwood tree and watch the kaleidoscope of the western sky as thin clouds and dust from the wheat harvesters play abut the setting sun to create a fantasia of roses, lavenders, and golds. I muse that if one were to capture these colors on canvas, critics would reject it as unrealistic and flashy. Over the ridge to the south of me runs a ravine dressed here and there by sumac, some wild bayberry still trying to lay claim to a territory, and a clump now and then of elderberry. Just beyond the limestone shelf the terrain levels off for a stretch and creates a meadow of native prairie grass. Close to its northern boundary is a buffalo wallow, still retaining its identity despite the cutting winds from the south, the rains, and the absence of buffalo. Strange, I've often thought, how the grass still refuses to grow in the wallows almost a hundred years after the passing of their creators. Drop south to the ravine again and follow its roll to the East, and one soon comes to the ridge of stone juttings that mark the farthest invasion west of the Flint Hills. There, at its face, can be found the scraps of flint left by the Cherokee spear and arrowhead chippers. On a good day one can occasionally find a perfect arrowhead, buried for decades but now exposed by the wind and rain.

The sky darkens into deeper reds and golds. The nearby Osage orange tree is silhouetted against the backdrop of the shifting western sky. I become still and sense the soft pulsations of the aged tree. During a brief interlude of time I envision myself becoming one with its life, my branches reaching out and up, searching for space, wanting to become more; my stalwart trunk braced for any of nature's surprises; my roots probing for food and moisture and possibly the unknown. I try to enter its life of earth and sky, not abandoning myself nor asking the tree to become me, just exchanging our separateness for a pause in joined existence. We have succeeded, for the moment was ours; we have failed, for we are alone again. Someday soon, we'll try again.

I walk along the old cattle trail toward home, remembering that White Bear told me that I could learn the ways of the Native Americans not from books or from the citizens of the nations but from their teachers— the wind, the sky, the creatures—and only when attuned in silence with the Great Spirit. The Indian tells us that if we wish to dance with wolves, rather than experiencing them as life separate from ourselves, we first find them within ourselves. Then the dance can begin.

5

The Enchanted Garden

🌹

Some farmers can feel or smell the soil and tell you what fertilizers it needs. Some gardeners can will a sick plant back to health, and some horticulturists know that love for their plants is more effective than their associates' cornucopia of chemicals. Beyond their affection and respect for the citizens of the plant kingdom is a reverence for the plants' essence that they experience as being at one with themselves.

This was the case with my neighbor, L. R. Trego, who had an uncanny relationship with plants. Machines, on the other hand, were his enemies. He seemed always to be in the midst of some war with his farm equipment. The warring parties occasionally struck an uneasy truce, during which time a degree of work was accomplished between them.

Machines seemed to stand between Trego and his soil, plants, and animals. Somehow, the machines didn't

interact with him appropriately—with sensitivity—and
the old farmer resented this. He couldn't look them in
the eye or reach out a hand to touch them and expect a
civil response. The machines appeared equally suspi-
cious of him, and their behavior—breaking down when
most needed—left something to be desired by even the
most patient of operators. Perhaps their conduct was
their way of responding to his insensitivity to their tech-
nical needs, usually met with a piece of baling wire and a
pair of pliers or even an indifference that prompted him
to pour water into the gas tanks. What co-existence was
possible between Trego and his mechanical assistants
was maintained with tension and ill-feeling. When he
couldn't handle the tractor's arrogance and the offset dis-
c's hydraulic petulance, Trego would harness up old Ben
and Bess and take to the fields with a simple, non-rebel-
lious harrow in tow. Using this traditional mode of
working the fields called forth from the farmer one of the
mountain songs of his youth.

As kids living on the next farm, we would giggle
over Old Man Trego's running battles with trucks, trac-
tors, wheat drills, and combines. Even his car appeared
to be having a difficult time adjusting to the width of the
garage. But there was no doubt in anyone's mind that
the old gentleman understood plants and animals better
than anyone else in the region. If your corn or your
peach tree required a diagnostician, Trego was the person to contact. And if your dog or horse was off his feed
or just seemed despondent about something, Trego
would visit with him and tell you what was wrong.

When our cattle or horses broke through a fence and
ran loose, we had to round them up. When Trego's live-

stock breached a fence, it was usually because they were looking for him.

Although our farms were located in a wheat and cattle region of Kansas, with the soil and the amount of rainfall dictating the choice of crops, Trego seemed to be able to grow anything. He and his wife always had a profusion of vegetables and fruits to share with their less-talented neighbors. Trego was the friend of man, beast, and plant, and was never one to withhold kindness from living things. Yet, he himself remained an enigma. His neighbors knew he had attended some excellent East Coast schools, had been a medical student somewhere, and had traveled widely, but they were never sure where. Many held his knowledge in awe. While they benefited from it now and then, they were content to accept it and him as a mystery.

Years later when I and the rest of the world marveled at the story of Findhorn Gardens, I found myself thinking that Old Man Trego would understand, and I wished that he was still around so that I could ask him about the magic of it all. I feel certain that the old farmer would agree that what happened and is happening at Findhorn is important. There, on a barren Scottish coast, three persons learned to communicate with the living spirits of plants and turned unproductive land into a garden that claims international attention.

The Findhorn happening started unfolding one cold November day in 1962 when Peter Caddy, his wife Eileen, and their friend Dorothy Maclean felt guided, for reasons to be made clear only later, to abandon their comfortable and successful lives and move to a remote corner of northern Scotland.

Caddy, who had been a high-ranking Royal Air Force officer and was the successful manager of plush resort hotels, answered the call of a powerful creative force revealed to him by his clairvoyant wife. They were told to leave everything behind them and move to an area called Findhorn Caravan Park. They had passed this place on their visits to Forres: a barren spot of wind-blown gorse and sand over looking the Firth of Moray and some three miles from Duncan's Castle, where the witches prophesied to Macbeth that he would be Thane of Glamis and Cawdor. The Caddys had always hurried past this unsightly sprawl of crowded mobile homes.

But listening to the voices of their souls, there they were, with their three sons and Dorothy Maclean, who had left a good position with the Canadian Foreign Office to join them, with no jobs, no prospects, and just their faith that somehow they would get through the winter. That long winter, however, grew into seven years, during which the six of them lived in a thirty-foot mobile home.

Caddy had always wanted to raise a garden. He read everything he could on the subject and decided to give it a try. "However," he explained, "to create a garden there at Findhorn seemed as absurd as Noah building an ark where there was no water. We were situated on a narrow sandy penisula jutting into the North Sea waters of the Moray Firth and were exposed to near-constant winds from all sides, with only a belt of conifers to the west to provide shelter. Worst of all was the soil: just sand and gravel held together by couch grass."

Exchanging what soil he could find for the gravel, Caddy worked back and forth with his wheelbarrow.

"This involved an enormous amount of work," he stated, "but it had a spiritual as well as a physical effect on the area. I was told that by working in total concentration and with love for what I was doing, I could instill light into the soil." Caddy says he felt radiations of light and love passing through him as he worked: when he started digging, energy flowed through him into the soil.

Once Caddy had taken action, some uncanny events began to unfold. A horse farmer offered him manure, the area's grass cuttings were made available to him, lumber came his way—as did much-needed cement—and he was given compost and straw bales to work into his sparse soil. Working day and night, he got the soil sufficiently prepared that spring to plant a number of vegetables and fruits.

This was the beginning of a legend. By the end of summer the settlers had preserved a number of different berries and put up nearly a hundred pounds of jam. They pickled cabbage and a large quantity of cucumbers. In a garage constructed with the lumber given them, the group stored potatoes, carrots, shallots, garlic, beets, and onions. During that winter they prepared the soil for additional planting, and by late spring they had planted more than twenty species of fruit trees and bushes.

The following year the yield of fruit and vegetables was unbelievable, with some of the produce reaching enormous size. Although the Caddys and Maclean lived according to the guidance they received on a daily basis about everything from inner development to the food they should eat and specific tasks they should perform, the trio realized that with the record-breaking success of their garden, some greater purpose was being played out at Findhorn. They speculated that what was happening was a pioneering project that could serve as a model to all mankind.

Then another breakthrough occurred: Dorothy Maclean, during meditation, received a message that enabled her to contact a spirit of the plant kingdom, one she identified as being the deva of the garden pea. The group did not reject this experience, for during their spiritual training they had learned that devas were part of the angelic hierarchy that maintains the archetypal pattern for each plant species. They accepted devas or nature spirits as an integral part of the creative process.

Caddy had for some time been interested in finding a way to cooperate with nature spirits. "Now, here was the pea Deva offering to help us in our garden," he wrote in *The Findhorn Garden*, adding, "I jumped at the chance, thinking: At last! Now we can get straight from the horse's mouth the answers to any questions we have on gardening. . . ."

Caddy assembled all questions that had stumped the group during the period when their gardens started to grow, and Maclean put these questions to the devas of the various plants. "Strange as it may seem," Caddy said, "we received the answers. Practical answers to practical questions."

Visiting scientists investigating the still-thin soil of the Findhorn community declared that the success the group was realizing with crops was impossible.

During the spring of 1964, when the county horticultural adviser arrived to run a soil analysis, he told the Caddys that the soil would require a dressing of at least two ounces of sulfate of potash per square yard. Caddy's response was that he didn't believe in artificial fertilizers and he would continue using compost and wood ash. The adviser told him that this approach would be totally inadequate.

When the county adviser returned with the soil analysis six weeks later, however, he acknowledged with considerable bewilderment that the analysis had revealed no deficiencies whatever. Even the necessary trace elements were present.

In the meantime, Dorothy Maclean had learned from the aeromatic plants in the garden that their wavelengths could serve special functions for humans. These effects had to do with different parts of the human anatomy as well as the human psyche, and that some plants were good for eyesight, others for wounds, others for emotions, and so on. It became clear to her that human passion, thinking, anger, kindness, and affection have far-reaching effects on the plant kingdom and that plants are most susceptible to human thoughts and emotions, which affect their energy. Anger and despondency have a detrimental effect on plants, while joyful frequencies have a beneficial effect. It occurred to Maclean that bad effects could come back to humans as they ate the produce they had infected with bad vibrations.

Maclean realized that the most important contribution that a person could make to a garden—more important than water and fertilizer—was the radiation, such as love, one puts into the soil while cultivating it. Everything that comes into a human being through inspiration of one sort or another, she explained, goes out again, modified in wavelength, tone, and timbre by the will of the person involved.

During the spring of 1967 Eileen Caddy was told

that the garden was to be extended and made into a place of beauty with the planting of many kinds of flowers. At the same time, the center was to be expanded and new housing constructed. A vision Eileen had received on the group's arrival at Findhorn was beginning to materialize. The money to build cedarstrip bungalows turned up as if by a miracle, and they were soon surrounded by beautiful flower gardens.

Findhorn was visited in 1968 by a number of garden and agriculture experts. All were amazed at what they found, and several remarked that they had never seen such a uniformly high standard of growth in all sections of the garden. The growth of the vegetables, flowers, and herbs was so remarkable that the visitors were at a loss to understand the phenomena, considering the harshness of the weather and the poverty of the soil.

Mrs. Elizabeth Murray, a well-known organic gardener and a member of the Soil Association, declared that the radiant health of the trees, flowers, fruit, and vegetables at Findhorn was far beyond the ordinary. She said that the compost was of such poor quality when mixed with sand that it could not explain the excellent produce, which for size, quality, and flavor was superior to anything she had ever seen anywhere. She was quite certain that such results could not have been attained on such barren soil and in such bleak weather simply by compost and good gardening.

Lady Mary Balfour, an accomplished organic gardener, spent a day and night at Findhorn in September of 1963 and wrote: "The weather throughout was grey and at times wet. Yet in retrospect I can see that garden in brilliant sunshine without a cloud in the sky, which must be due to the extraordinary brilliance of the blooming flowers I saw there. The flower beds were all a compact mass of color."

Professor R. Lindsay Robb, an agricultural expert for the United Nations, visited Findhorn shortly before Christmas in 1968, and he marveled, "The vigor, health and bloom of the plants in the garden at midwinter on land which is almost a barren powdery sand cannot be explained by the moderate dressings of compost, nor indeed by any known cultural methods or organic husbandry. There are other factors, and they are vital ones."

During this same time the Caddys and Dorothy Maclean were visited by Sir George Trevelyan, founder of Attingham College, who established the Adult Education Foundation in England. Sir George described sitting on a lawn "among daffodils and narcissi as beautiful and large as I have ever seen, growing in beds crowded with other flowers. I was fed on the best vegetables I have ever tasted. A young chestnut tree eight feet high stood as a central focus feature, bursting with astonishing power and vigor. Fruit trees of all sorts were in blossom—in short, one of the most vigorous and productive small gardens I have ever seen, with a quality of taste and color unsurpassed.

"I make no claim to be a gardener," he continued, "but I am a member of the Soil Association and interested in the organic methods and have seen enough to know that compost and straw mulch alone mixed with poor and sandy soil is not enough to account for the garden. There must be, I thought, a 'Factor X' to be taken into consideration. What was it?"

Caddy decided to level with Sir George and told him that the "Factor X" was their cooperation with the nature spirits. Sir George, long a student of the arcane and familiar with the work of George Washington Carver, Luther Burbank, Rudolph Steiner, and others, found no difficulty in accepting this explanation. Further, he was prepared to give it credence and to validate it by suggesting conscious investigation of such phenomena.

Trevelyan supported Caddy's position by pointing out that the ancients accepted the kingdom of nature spirits as a part of their everyday experience. He suggested that people's organs of perception of the super-sensible world may have atrophied as a result of the evolution of the analytical mind. "The nature spirits may be just as real as they ever were," he said, "though not to be perceived except by those who can redevelop the faculty to see and experience them."

Trevelyan went further. He thought the work at Findhorn had far-reaching implications, for the world's environmental situation was critical. He declared that "The world of nature spirits is sick of the way man is treating the life forces. The devas and elementals are working with God's law in plant growth. Man is continually violating it. There is real likelihood that they may even turn their back on man whom they sometimes consider to be a parasite on Earth. This could mean a withdrawal of life force from the plant forms, with obviously devastating results."

Sir George also called for others to copy the work done at Findhorn: "If this can be done so quickly at Findhorn, it can be done in the Sahara," he asserted. "If enough men could really begin to use this cooperation consciously, food could be grown in quantity on the most infertile areas."

Today Findhorn is known worldwide as a magical place, a very special piece of Earth. It has developed into a community of many disciples, and both scientific and spiritual leaders serve as faculty for the educational programs or as week-long workshop leaders. Residential training programs are provided to a number of students, and a publication entitled *One Earth* has been published quarterly since the spring of 1977. What started out as a small, miraculous garden has turned into a center of light drawing visitors from all over the globe.

Visiting scientists have been impressed that the people at Findhorn have not abandoned good horticultural practices even though the direction of their efforts came not through science but through communication with nature spirits. The willingness of Findhorn gardeners to listen to nature is new to moderns, whereas archaic humans knew how to listen to the forces of nature, according to William Irwin Thompson, general editor of a Findhorn publication, who believes that at this time all archaic cultures—Tibetan, Hopi, Sufi, and Celtic—are returning because they contain the very consciousness needed for the present and the future.

Being able to see with more than physical eyes and to experience vibrations beyond the limits of the electromagnetic spectrum may go a long way in explaining the mysteries that escape the instruments of the physicists. The German scientist Gustav Theodor Fechner, whose 1848 book, *Nanna, or the Soul-Life of Plants,* described his animistic vision of plants, now seems closer to reality. Burbank's insistence that whatever man wishes he can produce with the assistance of nature and George Washington Carver's belief that nature spirits abound in

the woods and take part in the growth of plants—these
ideas seem to warrant serious scientific investigation
rather than mere tolerance.

The message heard at Findhorn first by Peter and
Eileen Caddy and Dorothy Maclean and then by thousands of others is now being delivered in other parts of
the world. Among those listening is Machaelle Small
Wright. She is a nature researcher, teacher, flower
essence practitioner, and co-founder of Perelandra, a
twenty-acre nature research center in the Virginia countryside. In her book, *Behaving as If the God in All Life
Mattered,* she contends that she survived an early life of
torment and isolation through her communication with
the world of nature spirits and devas. Her reading of the
Findhorn experience, followed by her visit there, gave her
the confirmation she needed to devote her life to working
with entities of the nature kingdom in plant research,
writing, and the teaching of nature.

It well may be that in order for us to change our relationship with our planet, we will have to reassess our
relationship with the world of nature spirits and be willing to recognize their intelligence. Wright states in the
introduction of her book that our willingness to seek a
relationship with the nature spirits depends on our
admitting first that there is a need for that relationship.

We have evolved a world of considerable expertise
and high technology. We have countless teams of highly
qualified research scientists dedicated to finding out how
to live a healthier life on a healed planet. "Yet, despite all
this earnest technology and research," Wright argues, "I
am saying that we now need to turn our attention to
nature itself, recognize the intelligence inherent in all

nature forms on Earth and allow it to teach us what we need to know in order that we may apply that information to our life and our technology, and pull ourselves out of the present ecological mess."

Contact with a non-physical spiritual guide completely changed the life of author-publisher Meredith L. Young-Sowers, as she explained in her book, *Agartha*. Following considerable instruction in matters pertaining to her own spiritual life and growth, she was told to plant a garden and that this experience would bring her into a greater understanding of the intelligence present in all life forms.

During this period of guidance, her teacher, whom she always addressed as "Mentor," told her that the times of interaction with nature's life forces comes when the desire for oneness is sought openly through love. "These fleeting exposures to the plant and animal worlds occur when protective mental defenses are down and when one is peaceful and filled with what might be called the assertive edge of consciousness, meaning a dynamically positive sense of reaffirmation of the oneness of all life," Mentor said.

It is important that imagination be integrated into one's experience if the world of nature spirits is to be discovered, Young-Sowers's teacher explained. "The desire to be a part of nature and to share in all that goes on around each person is to regain and treasure the sense of imagination and the core experience of the spirit of life," Mentor told her. Since planting her garden and opening herself to the spirits of the flowers, Young-Sowers has been instructed to publish a set of divination cards that feature gorgeous photos of flowers inspiring divine guidance for those asking questions about their lives.

Many years ago as a young newspaper reporter I experienced my own journey to the Garden of Eden. It was a lazy summer afternoon at the Wichita *Eagle,* and I was in need of an excuse to get out of the newsroom before the city editor dreamed up some social gathering for me to attend. I had heard of a farmer living a few miles south of the city who was doing some unusual things with plants. It seemed to be the perfect day to give him a call. He was home and invited me out.

That afternoon turned out to be one of the most unforgettable experiences of my life. The gardens of Ross Gosney did not belong there, for this was prairie grass country, a land of hot summer winds and chilling winter blasts. Grass belonged there, as did wheat, milo, and a few other hardy survivors. But banana trees, lemons, and Louisiana swamp cypress? Had I, like Dorothy, been transported by a Kansas twister to a strange and magical land?

A sixtyish, pleasant-faced man with a quizzical grin was shaking my hand. "Howdy," he said, "glad you could come. I get quite a few visitors, but none this afternoon, so it's a good time."

We walked around his property, he speaking of this tree, that bush as though they were old friends, and I bewildered and trying to figure out what planet I had landed on. This was unfamiliar territory, and I felt as though I had taken a vacation from reality. Citrus trees grew among the peaches and apples, tropical flowers flourished alongside the petunias, and a California redwood had already reached higher than the walnuts and pecans. These were not growing in an enclosed botanical garden, nor were trees and bushes sitting around in huge pots, to be rushed inside at the first warning of frost. They were rooted firmly in the earth, and it was obvious that most of them had been there for a while.

After a time, I managed to set aside my awe sufficiently to resume my role as a reporter. I asked him how he had been able to accomplish what seemed the impossible. Gosney spent some time telling me how he had started the plants in soil that was similar to that in which each species would normally grow, and while a plant was small he started to acclimate it to Kansas weather. With the banana trees, which were particularly vulnerable, he had persisted in bringing them in and out of the freezing temperatures (they were damaged but not killed) until they managed to survive the winter outside. Then, with a winter behind them, he planted the trees outside permanently. To some extent, this was the history of many of the species.

Gosney spoke of this process, the soil, his own fertilizer formulas, and his loving care.

I accepted his assertion that all of these factors played their roles. Yet there persisted a feeling that this was only a part of the story. When I pressed him, he said, "Well, I'm afraid that I'm going to tell you the same thing that I've been telling the people from the agriculture colleges—and there have been several—that I'm simply not ready to reveal everything I do. . . . Maybe some day, but not yet."

The way he said it—slow, calculating, determined—it was obvious that he had made this same staternent more than a few times previously. This particular mystery's solution was not going to appear in tomorrow's issue of the Wichita *Eagle*.

A few months later I shared this experience with the late United States Senator Frank Carlson, who told me that he was a good friend of Gosney and had on occasion brought back unusual seeds from various parts of the world and given them to Gosney.

Carlson agreed that there were more ingredients in Gosney's successes than fertilizer, acclimation, and loving care. He didn't know what it was, but he added thoughtfully: "I can tell you this—maybe it's a clue, maybe it isn't—but many years ago Gosney spent some time in Tibet. His business with the plants started after he returned to this country."

As with Caddy, who also spent time in Tibet, had Gosney learned to communicate with plants? Was he able to work with nature spirits? Pondering these questions, I kept remembering an older cousin who had flown the "hump" between India and China during World War II. He swore that he had repeatedly flown over lush Himalayan gardens at altitudes above sixteen thousand feet. Perhaps James Hilton's story of Shangri-la in *Lost Horizons* is not just a fantasy after all.

The underlying philosophy of the Caddys, MacLean, and the many persons who have helped make Findhorn an international success, along with such individuals as Trego and Gosney, who turned their own backyards into magical places, is that all life is one. These people did not accept a science that separated man from the earth and its plants, but, discovering that all life forms are part of a divine identity, they were able to offer others a more profound reality.

6

The Human–Dolphin Connection
❧

Discoveries in recent years about the high intelligence of dolphins and other cetaceans, along with their affinity for humans, have made us re-think our position on this planet. Instead of standing alone as the only creature of significant intelligence, we now find ourselves in the position of sharing with cetaceans such qualities as reason, love, kindness, and loyalty.

People have long hoped to discover in the universe other life forms with which we can communicate. But instead of existing light years away, these forms share the same neighborhood. Thanks to the patience of the dolphins and the insights of several persistent scientists, our dream of moving beyond that of trainer-animal relationships to interspecies communication has become a reality. The knowledge, however, that humans must share with other beings the claim of a high level of awareness and sensitivity forces us to take another look at all inhabitants of the earth and to realize that our environment is one in which survival cannot be divorced from interdependence. We all sing the Life Song, or else we accept the silence.

My first exposure to dolphins came in an enchanted garden of coral, seaweed, fish, and other marine creatures in which they all appeared to flow in a slow, rhythmic dance through liquid sunlight. I was entranced by the awesome beauty of this silent world, and any thought of danger was foreign to my captured mind.

But this reverie was aborted quite suddenly when I became aware of a large, torpedo-shaped presence approaching me. I was a neophyte to this world; since our move to Madeira Beach, Florida, less than a month before, I had several times explored the waters off our beach, but those were harmless dives in fairly shallow water, and nothing more exciting than finding a few unusual seashells had resulted. I was searching for something a little more breathtaking, and my spirit of adventure had brought on my state of intoxication; I lacked the seasoned diver's sense of caution.

My reaction upon seeing the dark intruder was to panic. "Shark!" exploded in my brain. Instead of stopping all movement, I immediately launched myself to the surface and struck out in a frenzied free-style. But within a few strokes my "vicious attacker" was swimming pleasantly alongside me. There, only far enough away to avoid being pommeled by my flaying arms and legs, was a dolphin. We had daily watched playful schools of these magnificent dancers off our shore during the early morning hours, but this was my first closeup encounter, and this dolphin was so close there was no mistaking its identity.

Fear gave way to relief and more than a little awe as I slowed my eggbeater style of propulsion to a reasonable pace. The large dolphin stayed with me for a few yards and then, perhaps satisfied that I was okay, disappeared into deeper water. Needless to say, my experience was the primary substance of my conversations for the next couple of days.

Dolphins continued to remain a source of interest to us during our year on the island. We would occasionally encounter them on our swims, and they always engendered within us a sense of safety and comfort. Now and then they would feel playful, as one did the evening a friend kept getting butted from behind each time he tried to stand up in five-foot water. They could also be helpful: an elderly man living down the beach enjoyed having the sea's motion draw him on his inflated innertube to a distance off shore because he knew that, like clockwork, when he reached a certain point a dolphin would push him back to shore. "He depends on it, and they never fail him," his wife told us. Now and then we would go to the marina at St. John's Pass to watch Paddy perform. What we enjoyed most of all about these trips was to go below and talk to the dolphin while she rested alongside the glass wall. Somehow we always felt the urge to talk to her, not knowing whether she heard our voices but being quite sure that Paddy watched us with her large, luminous eyes.

It seems safe to venture that anyone who has had any kind of an association with dolphins was changed by that experience. My recollections of Florida always seem tied somehow to the dolphins. Why is that? What exchange has taken place that it left such a permanent imprint?

A number of years ago a friend of mine, while vacationing on the West Coast, was asked by a trainer of dolphins and other cetaceans to "call the dolphins." She did, and the dolphins came. She has mentioned this experience to me several times, as though it carries a special place in her memories. Not infrequently, one reads or hears about someone's association with dolphins or whales changing the course of his or her life. New windows have opened for them. Such an experience happened this summer to a close friend: a successful teacher of stress reduction techniques to top-level executives, he now plans to return to school to study interspecies communication.

Although some critics might view these transformations as being quixotic, a number of those enamored are physical and behavorial scientists whose credentials are in good order. "My life was changed by contacts with dolphins and whales," psychologist Joan Ocean told me. In the introduction to her book, *The Dolphin Connection,* she calls them "my friends, and even teachers. They have been teachers in the truest sense of the word . . . they are living examples of a way of life that expresses joy, harmony and health."

During her many years of working with mentally disturbed adults and abused children, Ocean, who feels deeply for such people, often became discouraged. She meditated and prayed for better ways to help and inspire these troubled persons.

"When I experienced the profound and enriching changes occurring in my life after swims with dolphins," she explained, "I felt strongly that these experiences would be life enhancing for anyone who chose to interact with dolphins in this way."

Joan Ocean found that being with dolphins always led

to extensive soul-searching filled with the excitement of many wonderful possibilities. New decisions grew from optimism and joy. More than that, the feelings and choices did not dissipate with time; instead, they led to more freedom in her life and work. "If ever I begin to doubt my ability to fulfill my plans, another dip with the dolphins returns to me a positive perspective."

Ocean discovered in her contacts with dolphin trainers, ecologists, marine researchers, and others who interact with cetaceans that every one of them had experienced telepathic communication between dolphins or whales and themselves. For career or personal reasons, however, they prefer not to focus on those interactions, which are unsettling for them, because they represent the unknown.

Fascinating stories about the dolphin's genius, inventiveness, and interactions with humans in myriad ways is legendary. Dolphins have been called the intellectuals of the sea, and some have even wondered whether they are more intelligent than humans. They have proven themselves tolerant and attentive students of scientists' tests and techniques and then have turned the process around, becoming the teachers in ways that have astonished their human associates. Animal researchers Vincent and Margaret Gaddis propose that, barring possible contact with intelligences from outer space, our first complex conversations with nonhumans will likely be with dolphins.

It took a scientist with vision, Dr. John C. Lilly, to open the door to the possibility that some other creature might be the intellectual equal of humans and that communication with this creature might force humans to reassess their relationship with all living things.

Although dolphins have been venerated since ancient

times and have found their way into the myths of many
cultures, the modern respect for cetaceans did not unfold
until the United States Navy decided to study dolphins in
the hope of learning from the dolphin's efficient swimming skills how to design an improved submarine. The
study was placed under the direction of Dr. Lilly, a neuro-
physiologist. No one dreamed, including Lilly, how
important the discoveries would be.

Dr. Lilly had to use a computer to keep pace with
the dolphins. He found that their brains work incredibly
fast compared to humans'. Colin Taylor, curator of the
Port Elizabeth Oceanarium in South Africa, has estimated that dolphins' brains work sixteen times faster than a
human's, although he is unsure how much information
they retain. When Dr. Lilly placed an electrode in the
"pleasure center" of a dolphin's brain, the dolphin
learned in one try to turn on the switch producing the
current. Monkeys generally have to make several hundred tries to learn this technique.

In his book *Man and Dolphins,* Dr. Lilly tells how a
young dolphin wandered out of sight of his group and was
attacked by three sharks. The dolphin uttered a series of
distress signals: short twin whistles, the first rising sharply
in pitch and the second falling just as abruptly in pitch.
The effect was quite amazing. More than twenty dolphins
who had been carrying on a lively discussion immediately
stopped their conversation and raced toward the scene at
their top speed—about forty miles an hour. The male dolphins rammed the sharks without slowing their speed.
Soon the cartilaginous skeletons of the sharks were shat-
tered, and they sank lifeless to the bottom of the sea.
Meanwhile, the females went to the assistance of the badly

injured young dolphin. He could not surface by means of his own strength, and two of the females placed themselves on either side of him, put their flippers under him, and raised him to the surface so that his blowhole was above the water and he could breathe. This maneuver was carried out by an exchange of whistling signals. From time to time the females relieved one another. Dolphins have been known to give this kind of aid to an injured member for two weeks, day and night, until a full recovery is made.

The dolphin's brain attains a degree of specialization far beyond that of man, and German psychiatrist G. Pilleri claims that the superior status of the brain of humans is "beginning to be a matter of doubt." Physicist and biologist Leo Szilard predicted in *The Voice of the Dolphin and Other Stories* that if humans should ever learn to talk to dolphins, those "intellectuals of the sea would win all the Nobel Prizes for physics, chemistry and medicine, and the Peace Prize to boot."

Rather convincing proof that dolphins carry on actual dialogue was provided when Dr. Lilly experimented by separating a pair of dolphins in a pool by a panel of sheet metal. At first the dolphins produced a shrill concert of whistles; they could obviously recognize each other's sounds even though they could not see each other. They even tried to leap high enough to glimpse each other, but failed. They both fell into silence. After a time, however, the male started encouraging his mate to converse with him. He carried on quite an extensive monologue before she responded. When she finally did speak, the male kept silence until she had finished. The conversation continued for varying periods of time.

Dolphins have been found to be sensitive to sounds

up to 150,000 cycles per second and to emit sounds up to 120,000 cps. They produce two primary sounds, whistling noises and a series of rapidly-repeated clicks, with frequencies up to 120,000 cps. The clicks are used in echo location and are emitted most of the time.

Laboratory tests have shown that the sonar system of dolphins is better than that of bats. In order to test this, rubber cups were fitted over the dolphins' eyes so that they could not see. Despite being temporarily blinded, the dolphins swam around their tanks at high speed without bumping into obstacles.

Scientists say that the evolution of language goes hand in hand with the development of the cerebrum. The brain of the dolphin, in its size and makeup, is well adapted for the development of language. Of course, for language to develop there must be something to communicate. Neuroanatomical research has shown that dolphins absorb as much information through seeing and hearing as we can, and because they are social animals they certainly have as much to communicate as prehistoric people who very definitely had a language.

A third prerequisite for the development of language is some means of expression. The dolphin certainly has that.

Dr. Lilly found that dolphins employ frequencies four and a half times higher than those used by humans and that they manage four and a half times as much information per unit of time as we do. Because the dolphin has two separate sets of sound-producing apparatus, one in each half of its blowhole, and they can be used simultaneously, Dr. Lilly believes that the dolphin should be able to emit nine times as much information per unit of time as the human can.

Dr. Kenneth S. Norris at the Makapuu Oceanographic Institute in Hawaii permitted his Pacific dolphins to carry on a telephone dialogue with Atlantic members of the species in the marine laboratories in Miami. An underwater microphone, telephone cables, and an underwater loudspeaker were rigged for the occasion. The Pacific and Atlantic branches were certainly able to communicate. Moreover, each dolphin let the other finish speaking before replying.

Encouraged by the telephone project, two naval engineers, T. G. Lang and H. P. Smith of the United States Naval Ordnance Test Station in Pasadena, California, were inspired to further test the speaking proficiency of dolphins. A dolphin pair, Doris and Dash, were placed in two separate soundproof tanks and were provided with an underwater telephone. The experimenters were able to interrupt the telephone connection whenever they liked.

Expressing themselves very tersely, the dolphins alternated in exchanging sounds. Neither talked for more than five seconds at a time. If no reply was forthcoming, the other dolphin dropped into silence. At certain intervals the dolphins uttered a few sounds, perhaps to check whether the other was again on the phone. And whenever the connection failed to function, the dolphins showed themselves to be aware of it instantly.

Drs. John Dreher, William E. Evans, and J.H. Prescott of the Lockheed Aircraft Corporation used sensitive electronic devices to listen in on the conversations of five bottlenose dolphins. While the dolphins were away, the scientists placed fifteen buoys across the mouth of California lagoon where the dolphins made their home. When the dolphins returned from an extended expedition in the ocean, they sighted the buoys, turned away, and huddled at a safe distance, talking back and forth for a minute. Then one of the dolphins, acting as a scout, detached himself from the group and approached the buoys cautiously, moving from one to the next. When the dolphin returned to his companions, the group exchanged a shrill burst of whistles. Following this discussion, a second dolphin left to inspect the buoys. When that dolphin returned, there was a vehement exchange of whistling. Once their doubts were assuaged, all the dolphins moved silently and cautiously past the buoys and into the lagoon.

Several years ago the Associated Press reported from Moscow that a school of dolphins in the Black Sea requested help from a fishing vessel. The small boat was suddenly surrounded by a number of dolphins who proceeded to push the boat in the direction of a buoy. There Russian fishermen found a young dolphin caught in the buoy's anchor rope. The men were able to free the dolphin baby, and when they succeeded the dolphin troop let out what the fishermen interpreted as whistles of joy. The dolphins then escorted the fishing boat all the way back to port.

The accidental discovery that dolphins mimic human voices presented the exciting possibility of eventual communication between humans and dolphins. One day a dolphin imitated the sounds of Dr. Lilly's laboratory equipment, and when the scientist played a tape of the sounds at a quarter its normal speed, he discovered that after his own voice stated the tape footage, "three-two-eight" the dolphin instantly and clearly repeated those words in a high-pitched whistle. The discovery was confirmed when other tapes of what seemed to be squawks, clicks, and whistles were played at the slower speed and the imitation of the human voice emerged. Dr. Lilly found that the dolphins were repeating the sounds in the laboratory, including laughter, but were doing it at a rate eight times faster than human speech.

One cannot work with an enthusiastic dolphin for a half-hour of continuous high-speed vocal exchange day after day for months at a time, Dr. Lilly wrote, "without being convinced that the dolphin is trying to communicate. In addition, the dolphin is doing a better job of it than the human investigators. Dolphins can mimic and even use several physical features of human speech so well that it is uncanny to hear it."

Dr. Lilly conducted some experiments with a series of syllables. He spoke a number of these language sounds in a certain order to a dolphin named Elver. In eighty-two to ninety-two percent of instances, Elver repeated the correct sound in the right order for a series of ten—something extremely difficult for a human to duplicate.

Those who have worked with dolphins are quick to point out that dolphins love to mimic. Two reporters, Ola and Emily D'Aulaire, declare that the dolphins they encountered fell into that pattern. Whatever swimming and diving techniques the dolphins saw, they immediately copied. "This talent can be carried to extraordinary lengths," the writers stated. "In one instance, a trainer blew a puff of cigarette smoke against the window of an observation tank. A young dolphin darted to its mother, nursed briefly, and spit out a cloud of milk against the glass. It was copying the 'smoke.'"

At another aquarium, a researcher placed a television set so that it could be viewed by a dolphin. Shortly thereafter the dolphin was noticed swimming in tight circles. Ola and D'Aulaire described the dolphin's reaction to the TV program it saw: "It squeaked loudly, picked up a toy ball floating nearby and flung it repeatedly into the air. When the trainers hurried to the TV, they realized the dolphin was trying to imitate a baseball game, raucous crowd noises and all."

Louis Herman, psychologist and laboratory director at Kewalo Mammal Laboratory in Hawaii, tells of an experiment in which two of his colleagues offered a ball and a Frisbee to a dolphin. Specific sounds were assigned to each object so that they would be associated with those objects. The dolphins quickly learned to imitate each sound and associate it with the appropriate object. After a short time, when the trainers showed the dolphin a ball or a Frisbee, the animals would supply the correct sound.

At an aquarium in Hawaii, a team led by Dr. Gregory Bateson was able to teach a dolphin to perform new tricks, one after the other, in order to receive its reward. The dolphin not only understood what was required of it, it also showed great imagination and invention in adding to its repertoire.

There seems to be little doubt that dolphins learn quickly from observation. In the shows given at aquariums it sometimes happens that a dolphin expected to perform a certain trick for some reason fails to do so, and on a number of occasions another dolphin completely untrained for the trick steps in and performs it perfectly.

In another experiment in which a male and female dolphin were required to perform a trick quickly, they were presented with two keys and a signal light. When the light was steady they were to depress the key on the right; when it was blinking, the key on the left. Then they had to learn that the male was to press first. Further, a screen was placed between the animals so that only the female saw the signal light. When the first signal was given, the female swam up to her keys and uttered some dolphin sounds. The male then pressed the correct key of his pair, whereupon the female pressed the correct key on her side. The dolphins never failed to go through the sequence correctly.

Whatever their level of intelligence, dolphins are demonstrating great empathy and understanding of humans with special problems. They have been used to work with children and adults who have Down's syndrome, hydrocephalus, cerebral palsy, muscular dystrophy, and head and spinal injuries.

Fifteen dolphins are used by David Nathanson in this kind of therapy at Miami's Dolphin Research Center. "There's a rapport between these individuals and the dolphins which is difficult to explain. The dolphins are very gentle and seem to understand that these persons have special needs," he said.

When five-year-old Deane-Paul Anderson was first brought to Nathanson in 1989, the child was unable to speak a single word. He was born with Down's syndrome and had become a shy loner. Today, after weekly sessions with Nathanson and interactions in the water with dolphins, he is talkative and outgoing. His mother told writers Ola and D'Aulaire: "The dolphins unlocked a little door to his mind, and Deane-Paul bubbled out."

Patricia St. John, researcher and author of *Beyond*

Words, Unlocking the Secrets to Communicating, converses directly with dolphins and uses what she learns from them to help people with autism. St. John suggests that the secret of communicating is to approach all creatures on terms of equality and respect, with love and a willingness to learn from them, rather than expecting them to conform to our own verbal language.

As with complex human beings, dolphins are not easy to understand. One of the greatest puzzles is their affinity for humans despite the way we have treated them. Their friendliness toward human beings is legendary, as attested by many instances of dolphins allowing people to ride them through the waves for sport and dolphins rescuing people. In light of our having captured, persecuted, and killed dolphins, it is difficult to understand why the dolphins have remained friendly. Yet there is no record of a dolphin ever having injured a person, not even when that person is engaged in killing a dolphin.

With more than eighty percent of some species of dolphins killed and others facing similar fates in the fishing nets, we can't help wondering whether these caring creatures are too good for us. Maybe they won't be able to survive in the environment we have created for them.

Dolphins are born to bring love, life, and creativity to the oceans. They are manifested to form a bridge of joy and intelligence between the aquatic kingdom and the human kingdom, but since we will not allow them to do this, they are leaving the planet, Gary Zukav argues in *The Seat of the Soul.*

However, psychologist Joan Ocean, who spends a great deal of time with dolphins and other cetaceans, believes that the animals will stay, for they are encouraged by some of the breakthroughs in the relationship between themselves and some humans. In her experience the dolphins have a great deal to teach humans, and they are willing to do it. Ocean points out that a growing number of people are deeply concerned about the environment; they are finding ways to care for the Earth in the belief that their mission is to educate the greater population in the protection of the planet's soil, water, air, plants, and wildlife. One important source of knowledge and help, believes Ocean, is the large-brained whales and dolphins, who have lived peacefully in their environment for fifty million years without destroying the Earth. She contends that we can learn from them.

This communication with cetaceans is urgent, according to Ocean, for more and more people are beginning to realize that science and technology lack the answers for averting disasters. "The lucrative attraction for inappropriate technology has led to a life estranged from Nature, sanctioning the demise of our life-support systems," she states.

Ocean is convinced that "Dolphins have information that contains solutions for us." She says that dolphins will not, however, be teaching us in traditional ways. Instead, "Their communication-of-information challenges us to expand our intelligence capabilities" by using new bodily receptors. Such Dolphins, she points out, are not merely sending us information, "they are showing us an entirely new method of understanding, experiencing and interacting with our environment."

Ocean, who now lives in Hawaii, had her first experience with dolphins in Florida, where after swimming and playing with them, she felt surrounded by a deep sense of peace, and the world appeared vibrant and unusually beautiful; she was acutely aware of the sounds, sights, and smells around her. While swimming with the dolphins, she received volumes of information about the interdependence of the oceans and the earth, and it filled her awareness. She understood how carefully ecosystems were intertwined and interrelated and how every living thing has a purpose.

"I experienced a symbiotic love for the ocean," she said. "I felt protective of it. I accepted completely my personal connection to it, and my responsibility to preserve and respect all of the vast life forms that resided within it."

The information came to her by what she refers to as "absorption." It was not intellectualized, nor was it visualized in words or images, but it was felt. It was in some way absorbed into the fabric of her intelligence so that whatever previous knowledge existed within her "was incorporated into the new information and the ultimate understandings involved my knowledge of the cetaceans."

What are the experiences and discoveries of people like Lilly, Ocean, Bateson, and Nathanson telling us? Their experiences and studies reveal that we lack all the answers concerning the problems of the world in which we and other creatures live. What also seems obvious is that these answers cannot be located entirely in the domain of science and technology. Just as some scientists are now saying that the organic brain and the non-organic mind are not synonymous, so there are qualities of living systems responding to love, will, and exchanges that cannot be measured in the laboratory. We have gained at least a small understanding of the attributes of certain types of intelligence, but it would be arrogant of us to believe we know the source, nature, and attributes of all possible intelligences. And it is unlikely that we will, for the intelligence that would make such an encompassing discovery would itself be changed by this event.

What we do know is that the John Lillys of the world are to be commended for having the courage to face us with new questions. In the search for the solutions as to the nature, roles, and potentialities of cetaceans and the possibility of interspecies communication, we are certainly learning something about dolphins and whales. We may even be humbled somewhat by our investigations and, to best-case our experiences, we might expand our states of awareness.

If we are to find solutions to our problems, we will need to develop greater understanding than we have so far demonstrated. If we accept what Lilly and his fellow pioneers are proposing, the dolphins and whales are standing by to help in this pursuit.

7

Nature's Secret Signals

🌿

"A life signal may connect all creation," Cleve Backster told my friend Marcel Vogel and me. "That may sound like an earth-swallowing statement, but I believe in can be demonstrated."

"I have no doubt about that," Marcel Vogel commented slowly, thoughtfully. "When we get back to the hotel, why don't you guys come to my room for a few minutes? I have some materials I want to show you."

The three of us fell silent for a few minutes, caught up in our own thoughts and the magic of a perfect late Los Angeles night in April. It had been a day of considerable mental adventure, for we had spent the preceding fifteen hours with the other members of the Ernest Holmes Research Foundation, a group established to examine the evidence for non-traditional methods of healing. It included such exciting conversants as Dr. Carl Simonton, later to be internationally known for his work with cancer patients; Dr. Bill Tiller, Stanford physicist; Olga Worrall,

the healer; Dr. Ballantine Henley, president of the United
Church of Religious Science; Willis Kinnear, publisher of
Science of Mind magazine; Dr. Robert Miller, professor of
chemical engineering at Georgia Tech; and actors Robert
Young and Gloria Swanson.

When Vogel, Backster, and I left the group to take a
leisurely walk along Wilshire Boulevard back to our
hotel, we were talking about Backster's current research.
Vogel and I were highly curious about any new develop-
ments in the work of the man who had staggered the scientific community and delighted gardeners everywhere
by announcing that plants respond to emotional stimuli.

But it had been a long day, and rather than get into a
heavy discussion we started laughing over some of the
jokes made by the news media about Backster's findings,
such as the story of the man whose excuse for not cutting
his lawn was that he didn't want to hurt the feelings of
the grass. We laughed, did a few impromptu dance steps
on the boulevard, and before long were hugging trees
and hollering at each other to check out the energy field
of first this tree and then another. We decided it was
nice to be alive and to have such friends as Eucalyptus
and Bougainvillea.

Back at the hotel, Vogel, then senior chemist at IBM
in San Jose, California, confessed that Backster's experiments had led him into new fields of research. What he
wanted to show us were pictures of two leaves. Both
leaves, he explained, were picked from the same plant
and at the same time. The first leaf was brown and dehy-
drated; it had been ignored after it was picked. The second leaf was green and fresh. He said he had kept it that
way by willing it to remain so.

It may be somewhat disconcerting to learn that the philodendron plant sitting in your kitchen window screams silently when you break an egg in the frying pan, or that the potted gardenias on the sun porch grow fearful whenever your dog walks by. Further, it is a bit of a thought-teaser to be told that when you accidentally cut your finger the dying cells in the drying blood transmit recordable signals to the philodendron and the gardenias.

Provocative statements? Yes, indeed, but ones that continue to be taken seriously and investigated quietly by scientists at several major universities since Backster made his ground-breaking report more than twenty-five years ago.

Backster's thesis: To discover if there is an unknown link between the cells of plants and animals that transmit distress signals revealing threats against any member of the living community.

These startling implications were reported in an abstract published on September 7, 1967, by Backster, a former interrogation specialist with the Central Intelligence Agency, a consultant to almost every government agency using a polygraph (popularly known as a lie detector), and a designer of polygraph procedures used by law enforcement agencies throughout the country.

This is what happened one morning in Backster's laboratory:

Immediately following the watering of an office plant, he wondered if it would be possible to measure the rate at which water rose in a plant from the root area to the leaf.

He decided to try it by using electrodes and attempting to measure on the polygraph the increase in the plant leaf's moisture content. He used a nearby Draena Massangeana plant, securing the electrodes with a rubber band. But "contrary to my expectation, from the outset the plant leaf tracing exhibited a downward trend. Then, after about one minute of chart time, the tracing exhibited a contour similar to a PGR traction pattern typically demonstrated by a human subject experiencing an emotional stimulation of short duration."

As he watched the PGR tracing, he wondered if there could be a similarity between the tracing of the plant and one from a human. "I decided to try to apply some equivalent to the threat-to-well-being principle, as a well-established method of triggering emotionality in humans. I first tried to arouse the plant by immersing a plant leaf in a hot cup of coffee. But there was no measurable reaction.

"After a nine-minute interim, I decided to obtain a match and burn the plant leaf being tested. At this instant of this decision . . . there was a dramatic change in the PGR tracing in the form of an abrupt and prolonged upward sweep of the recording pen. I had not moved, or touched the plant, so the timing of the PGR pen activity suggested to me that the tracing might have been triggered by the mere thought of harm I intended to inflict on the plant. This occurrence, if repeatable, would tend to indicate the possible existence of some undefined perception in the plant." What Backster had discovered is that if you decide to hurt your plant, it will show fear.

Backster was to find that his plants were in communication with other life forms and would record the moment that fertile eggs or brine shrimp were placed in boiling water. Plants were not, however, the only monitors of life's signals, and he discovered responses from the most primitive unit of life. This applied even to bacteria, and he began to refer to this phenomenon as "primary perception below the cellular level."

The *Wall Street Journal* reported that Backster's experiments "seem to indicate that besides some sort of telepathic communication system, plants also possess something closely akin to feelings or emotions. . . . They appreciate being watered. They worry when a dog comes near. They faint when violence threatens their own well-being. And they sympathize when harm comes to animals and insects close to them."

Backster explained how his plants responded to his dog's anxiety over an alarm in his office. He kept a Doberman Pinscher in a back room, where an electric timer was hooked to a loud alarm directly above the dog's bed. About five seconds before the alarm rang, a barely audible click could be heard. The dog hated the sound of the alarm, so when he heard the click he left the room before the alarm sounded. Although Backster slept in a different room, he knew exactly when the dog was leaving the room, even though he could not hear the click, because the plants acknowledged the dog's movements by reacting to the dog's anxiety that began when the click sounded.

The one thing that rubber tree plants, brine shrimp, dogs, and eggs have in common are cells, so responses must occur at a cellular level. Because of this link, biologist Lyall Watson suspects that these responses are applicable to all life forms. He suggests that the signals began as comparatively simple patterns of communication between single cells within a single organism, possibly before the development of a proper nervous system. Watson points out that some plants without coordinating nerve networks can still orchestrate their cells into such precise harmony that thousands will respond simultaneously with a movement fast enough to catch a fly. While this mechanism still remains a mystery, the biologist wonders if Backster hasn't found the answer.

Watson speculates if the next stage could have been for cells, such as pollen grain or sperm, to carry this sensitivity beyond the boundaries of the organism to produce new entities that could establish an independent existence and nevertheless maintain contacts with others of their kind. It is possible, he suggests, that compromise signals were developed among groups of closely related species, perhaps in response to a common predator. The predator would then find it necessary to tune in to the same wavelength in order to detect the signals and thus anticipate their effect on the behavior of its prey. Finally, both predator and prey could use the signal to give warning of some natural catastrophe that could affect them all. "This scenario for the development of what Backster calls primary consciousness in all living things is purely theoretical," Watson states, "but it is the kind of path that evolution often takes. It is seldom that a need is allowed to exist for very long without nature taking some steps to meet it."

Watson believes that "If a network of communication does exist between all living things, one would expect to see it most dramatically manifest in times of crisis. Spontaneous human telepathic contacts most often occur when one of the people involved is in danger or dying. The death signal may be just the 'loudest sound' in this universal language and therefore the one first to come to our attention. There is evidence to show that it is more than just a simple on-off alarm system."

When we met at the conference Backster told Vogel and me that the nature of this death signal is still a riddle. Nothing appears to prevent it from reaching its intended goal. "It does not appear to be within the known frequencies, and it does not take a form that can be shielded by ordinary means." He has tried without success to prevent electrical penetration by shielding the plants with a Faraday screen and even lead-lined containers, but the signal "is not within any known portion of the electromagnetic spectrum, and distance does not seem to have a bearing."

Backster would like to get the space scientists to use a space probe to prove that distance doesn't limit primary perception. He suspects that a plant wired to a polygraph on a space satellite attuned to a person at Ground Control at Houston would react nearly instantaneously if some unusual emotion occurred. If it did, Backster believes, the experience would give evidence supporting a non-time-consuming form of communication, a phenomenon not falling within the electromagnetic spectrum—at least, as we now understand it.

When it became apparent to Backster that plants were capable of establishing a rapport with their owners, he began making notes of his actions, timing them with a stop watch when he was away from the laboratory. He would invariably find upon his return that any agitation he had experienced, whether it was irritation with a newsstand vendor or fright at almost being hit by a car, had registered on the plants' polygraph. He also found the plants' greatest emotional response occurred when he thought of returning to his office, regardless how far away he was when he had the thought.

Dr. Robert Miller, a member of the Ernest Holmes group, watched Backster give a striking demonstration for an Atlanta audience of the way plants identify with their owners. Miller described for me how Backster "delicately clamped two stainless steel electrodes to one of the broad leaves" of a plant owned by a member of the audience and hooked up his polygraph. The recorder pen began to oscillate and then drop, making a pattern that Backster says is typical of a "people trace." When the trace became steady (meaning the plant was comfortable), Backster asked the owner of the plant if he could make a light cut on the man's finger with a razor. The plant was six feet away from the owner, and as Backster approached him with the razor, the plant "registered the man's apprehension." When the cut was made, the plant showed little response, but when the iodine was applied to the wound, "the recorder pen oscillated violently. Cleve's explanation was that living cells were being destroyed by the iodine and the plants were aware of their death."

With his discovery of a plant's sympathetic reaction to its owner, Backster wondered if a plant would react to the death of another plant. In the resulting experiment, Backster proved that plants can identify the killer of another plant!

To carry out this dramatic experiment, he put two plants in a room and blindfolded six volunteers in another. Each volunteer drew a slip of paper from a hat. One slip of paper was marked for murder: a volunteer who drew it was to tear one plant out by the roots, shred it, and stamp on it. The other slips directed the volunteers to follow different (non-lethal) directions.

Removing the blindfolds, each volunteer looked at his or her assignment and, one by one, left for the plants' room to follow instructions. Backster stayed in another part of the building and so did not know which of the six was slated to destroy the plant. When all six volunteers were collected together, Backster went into the room and hooked up to the polygraph the remaining plant, which was to act as a witness to the crime. Then each volunteer was brought before the plant. When the plant was confronted by the murderer, the polygraph needle jumped wildly.

Was it the man's guilt the plant was picking up, or did it actually recognize him? Backster sought all possible explanations. Then Backster wondered about the murdered plant: Had it picked up the man's intentions to kill, as the earlier threat-to-well-being experiment had suggested?

To learn whether plants pick up deadly intentions, Backster attached the electrodes to three vegetables. A volunteer was asked to pick up a vegetable and drop it into boiling water. The vegetable seemed to faint before it was even touched! The volunteer's plan to kill it registered on the polygraph by a sudden upward bound followed abruptly by a straight line—an effect that suggests loss of consciousness.

Biologist Lyall Watson describes a study conducted several years ago by the Institute of Psychological Sciences in Moscow in which plants responded to a volunteer's emotional states. A woman named Tanya was chosen for the experiments because she seemed to be able, under hypnosis, to produce on demand apparently real emotions like fear, happiness, anger, and grief. "She was placed just eighty centimeters from a flowering geranium connected to an electroencephalograph," Watson relates. "During the series of tests, when Tanya shivered with cold, cringed with fear, laughed with joy, or cried with sadness, the plant produced a whole range of electrical responses in time with her behavior. She could never produce any response on the machine when the plant was not present and the readings obtained from the electroencephalograph could not be attributed to stray electrical interference because the plant-instrument combination was kept running in the gaps between her emotional displays."

Apparently, plants can also detect lies. When Tanya, under hypnosis, was asked to think of a number between one and ten and told never to reveal it, a new experimenter trying to elicit the number counted slowly from one to ten. Although she answered each number with a decisive no, the flower identified the lie and the chosen number by responding only to the number she had chosen (five).

Interspecies communication of an unusual nature was demonstrated a number of years ago by Dr. Olga Worrall, an internationally known healer and associate director of the New Life Clinic of the Methodist Church in Baltimore. Dr. Robert Miller, an Atlanta chemical engineer and former professor at Georgia Institute of Technology, wondered if Dr. Worrall could communicate with plants at some distance and even enhance their growth rate, so he set up a rotary electrochemical transducer and strip chart recorder in order to measure plant growth rate. He asked Dr. Worrall to pray for and send energy to the plants from her home in Baltimore, some 600 miles away. During an eleven-hour period, the plants grew at the rate of 52.5 millimeters per hour—more than 800 percent the normal rate!

Plants evidently emit some sort of beams not unlike ultraviolet light. A number of years ago Russian scientist Dr. Alexander Gurvich declared that "All living cells produce an invisible radiation." He claimed to have found rays that he named "mitogenetic radiation" coming from plants. He supposedly demonstrated that radiation from the tip of an onion root bombarded the side of another onion root and caused a marked increase in growth. The strange radiation increased the growth of bacteria and yeast also, but the energy reaction was stopped by glass. Ordinary glass filters out ultraviolet light; quartz glass, on the other hand, allows ultraviolet rays to penetrate, and when quartz plates were used the rays were not inhibited. Gurvich discovered mitogenetic rays coming from people, too, and claimed that illness altered the radiation. He found that when a sick person holds yeast culture in his hands even briefly the cells are killed.

Gurvich's work was performed in the 1930s and seemed to hold great promise for medicine, yet it faded when he failed to produce a theory. But his work was not forgotten. Currently, Russian biophysicists are taking another look at Gurvich's work. At Moscow University Dr. Boris Tarusov has found that plants modulate their light and radiate signals bearing certain messages, including advance warnings of disease. The Russians have found that light waves appear to carry information from one group of living cells to another at a distance and that this communication appears to be carried out by means of the ultraviolet band.

Another Russian scientist, Dr. Victor Adamenko,

suggests, as does Backster, that the signal may move on a carrier wave beyond the electromagnetic spectrum. "Experiments appear to show that plants receive some kind of emanation at a distance of a hundred miles and that known methods of screening from electromagnetic waves do not prevent the plant from receiving the signal," Dr. Adamenko states.

Vogel, who has now become an internationally recognized expert on liquid crystals, wondered if the energy that kept a leaf alive could affect liquid crystals. To work on his theory he took hundreds of color slides of liquid crystal behavior magnified three hundred times. He concluded that crystals are brought into a solid or physical state by pre-forms or ghost images of pure energy, which anticipate the solids. As plants could pick up the intentions of humans, so Vogel was equally convinced that intent produced some kind of energy field.

To demonstrate the role that he played personally in his experiments, Vogel hooked two plants to the same recording machine. From the one plant he tore off a leaf, and the second plant responded to this "hurt"—but only when he paid attention to it. It became clear to Vogel that a certain state of consciousness on his part was an integral part of the circuitry in monitoring his plants.

Vogel tells his audiences that a life force, or cosmic energy, surrounding all living things is shareable among plants, animals, and humans. "It seems," he told me, "that I act as a filtering system which limits the response of the plant to the outside environment. I can turn it off or on, so that people and plant become mutually responsive. By charging the plant with some energy within me, I can cause the plant to build up a sensitivity for this kind of work. It is extremely important that one understand that the plant's response is, in my opinion, not that of an intelligence in plant form, but that the plant becomes an extension of myself. . . ."

This position highlights the difference in approaches between Vogel and Backster. Vogel is concerned with the human control of the plant, whereas Backster contends that his plants, left alone, will react to their environment on their own. Quite possibly they are to some degree both correct. But the question one immediately raises about Backster's position is whether an experimental plant is ever alone. It may be that plants not under human scrutiny react to their environment without any help from human beings; yet there is no way that we can measure this interaction, because the moment we become interested in the matter we have contributed to the action.

It seems clear that the relationship of plants to humans is a vital component in successful experiments. Speaking of researchers who have endeavored to elicit electrical responses from plants and other living organisms by means of emotional and mental stimuli, Vogel stated: "Hundreds of laboratory workers around the world are going to be just as frustrated and disappointed as these men until they appreciate that the empathy between plant and human is the key, and learn how to establish it. No amount of checking in laboratories is going to prove a thing until the experiments are done by properly trained observers. Spiritual development is indispensable. But this runs counter to the philosophy of many scientists, who do not realize that creative experimentation means that the experimenters must become part of their experiments."

Plants, then, must have a certain form of consciousness. "All life, within its own terms, reveals itself to be just as sensitive to suffering and thus threats-to-well-being as we are," Lawrence Blair states in *Rhythms of Vision.* "Vegetarians may now require other reasons for their dietary habits—and there are many others—than the belief that animals suffer and plants do not. Recognition of the 'emotional' or vibratory states of plants and animals—as well, of course, of humans—at the time of their death, has long been reflected in such religious practices as the Kosher 'quieting' rituals prior to the sacrifice of animals for food, or in the 'blessing' of crops before they are harvested."

This view of all life as consciousness raises moral as well as biological questions. I for one now have a very difficult time cutting down live trees, but if it were taken to its logical limits we would end up, like the community in Samuel Butler's *Erewhon,* eating nothing but cabbages that have been certified to have died a natural death. Perhaps the answer to the moral question resides in treating all life with respect, and killing, with real reluctance, only that which is necessary for survival. This was and, to some extent, remains the position of Native Americans. The deer may be killed for food (goes the belief) but the hunter kills it with gratitude and respect. And, as mentioned earlier, Mad Bear asked that we not walk on the grass without thanking it for being there for us.

The biological problems raised by these experiments are not easily resolved. We can't help wondering why so many forms of life send out signals to their own as well as other species while we don't. Alarm signals appear to be common throughout the kingdom of nature, ourselves being the exception . . . or perhaps somewhere along the way it will be discovered that we, too, send out such signals. In the meantime, we'll have to muddle along with our phones and radio transmitters. Meanwhile, we're already aware of such alarm signals among other species. Seagulls have specific calls that warn their breeding colonies of the approach of predators. Ground squirrels and prairie marmots have an early-warning system that alerts their colonies to the danger of air raids by birds of prey. The function of the signals is so clear that those of crows and gulls have been recorded and broadcast across airfields to frighten these birds off the runways just before a plane is due to land. Very often the alarm is interspecific: terns, starlings, and pigeons feeding with gulls all take to flight at the sound of the gull alarm call, and seals dive into the water when nearby colonies of cormorants give notice of approaching danger.

"Love, hate, joy, fear, pleasure, pain, excitability, stupor, and countless other appropriate responses to stimuli are as universal in plants as in animals." Those are the words of Sir Jagadis Chandra Bose, who was the first scientist to attempt to assess the possibility of a universal language of life. Born in 1848, Bose was the first Indian to win distinction in modern science and ultimately international acclaim in physics, physiology, and psychology.

Bose first claimed the attention of the scientific community when he demonstrated that the boundary line between so-called "non-living" metals and "living" organisms was tenuous indeed. He began a comparative study of the curves of molecular reaction in inorganic substance and those in living animal tissue. He learned that the curves produced by slightly warmed magnetic oxide of iron showed striking resemblance to those of muscles. In both, response and recovery diminished with exertion, and the consequent fatigue could be removed by gentle massage or by exposure to warm water. Other metals also reacted in animal-like ways.

A short time later Bose theorized that if the striking parallels between such extremes as metals and animal tissue were real, he should also be able to get similar effects in plants, which, because they were believed to have no nervous systems, were universally considered to be unresponsive. Bose picked some horse chestnut leaves and discovered that they responded to "blows" in much the same manner as had the metal and muscles. Excited about this result, he bought some carrots and turnips. He found them to be highly sensitive. When he chloroformed plants, he discovered that they were as successfully anaesthetized as animals, and that when the drug vapor was dissipated by fresh air, like animals they revived.

With the ingenious development of his mechanical apparatuses for measuring and recording nervous impulses in animals, Bose proved that plants exhibit excitatory response to mechanical stimulation much as animals do.

By means of Bose's Resonant Recorder, by which he registered the speed of transmission of excitatory impulse, and the Oscillating Recorder, which traced the throbbing pulsations of the telegraph plant, he demonstrated the striking similarity of plant impulses to the pulse beat of the animal heart. Bose found, for example, that when a plant was pricked with a pin, its normal growth rate was immediately depressed to a fourth, and it took about two hours for the plant to recover from the wound.

With another apparatus, the Crescograph, Bose

could actually observe the small life-movements of a carrot. As a pair of forceps pinched it, the carrot's electric shudder of pain was seen on the screen. When a leaf of the telegraph plant was cut from the parent plant and the cutting placed in water, the leaflet's pulse ceased, and although after it renewed for a number of hours, it gradually grew weaker as it died. The sensibilities of the mimosa plant became paralyzed for several hours after a leaf was cut off. In *The Autobiography of a Yogi,* Paramahansa Yogananda tells of watching Bose jab a sharp instrument through a part of a fern. Looking at the magnified fern shadow on the screen, he saw it shake spasmodically at the moment of injury and then saw it die, trembling violently, as Bose partly sliced through the stem with a razor. The death contraction in the plant appeared to be in every respect like the death contraction in an animal.

It had been long believed that plants liked unlimited amounts of carbon dioxide, but Bose learned that too much of the gas might suffocate them. They could, however, be revived, just like animals could, with oxygen. Like human beings, plants became intoxicated when given shots of liquor. They swayed like drunks, passed out, and eventually revived, although with definite signs of hangover.

Upon his retirement, Bose summed up his scientific philosophy:

"In my investigations on the action of forces on matter, I was amazed to find boundary lines vanishing and to discover points of contact emerging between the living and the non-living. My first work in the region of invisible lights made me realize how in the midst of luminous ocean we stood almost blind. Just as in following light

from visible to invisible our range of investigation transcends our physical sight, so also the problem of the
great mystery of Life and Death is brought a little nearer
solution, when, in the realm of the Living, we pass from
the Voiced to the Unvoiced."

Bose's work forces us to consider whether there is
any possible relation between our own life and that of
the plant world. In any case, we need to abandon all our
preconceptions about lack of consciousness in the plant
world. The answers to questions about plants can be
found in only one way: we must ask the plant.

8

Primates Experience Life Much as Humans Do

❦

All brawn and no brain? I had heard the stories of how big he was, how he could collapse an eight-ply truck tire with one arm, how the walls shook as though caught in an earthquake when he threw his body against them. I was prepared to be impressed, but not at all in the way it happened. Visions of King Kong had come easily to mind; an image of a silent interrogator had not.

A holiday visit with relatives in Milwaukee afforded the opportunity to tour the city 's world-famous zoo and to see first hand its best-known citizen: Samson, the 600-pound male gorilla.

It was the middle of a mellow summer morning when we arrived, and the size of the crowd made one wonder if all the scout troops and visiting firemen had chosen this particular day for their outing. And Samson, living up to his tumultuous reputation, was claiming his share of center stage. He stalked his audience of galvanized children with the arrogance of a seasoned linebacker promising to dismantle a rookie quarterback. He would approach the thick glass wall separating him from his observers and strike the barrier with both fists, eliciting the complete attention of the elders and the squeals of the youngsters. Seeing the focus now riveted on him, he moved a number of feet away from the glass, then without warning hurled his massive weight against the glass.

It shuddered, a deep, significant shudder. The walls, the floor, the air itself shuddered, for Samson was making a statement. It was there for the children, briefly shrieking and then nervously propelled into hyper-laughter; there for the adults who gave a couple of feet of ground but could not surrender anything else in their relationship to him.

And me? I'm not sure about my experience. There was something I wanted to understand, and my emptiness searched for it. But transfixed in my position in front of the glass, I could only wait, as though the next lines in the script would reveal the real meaning in all this.

Only Samson seemed to understand, for he had played his role many times. He stalked away and then, in what appeared to be an afterthought, he picked up his truck tire and hurled it against the glass. He glanced back once at his audience, then moved to a far corner of his room and sat down. He stared at the floor, looked at the ceiling, but not again at the people. Their existence was no longer acceptable.

The crowd moved slowly away, seeking excitement elsewhere, or perhaps feeling mildly uneasy in the silence. I kept watching him, maybe hoping for a better resolution. And suddenly I realized his eyes were fixed on mine. The eyes weren't seeing me as his master, his superior; they weren't going to give me that. Samson didn't expect to receive more, and he wasn't offering more. The eyes made it clear that what we had was the extent of the exchange. I read a flicker of disdain in the black eyes, and they were holding me responsible. I, too, moved away, outside to where the giraffes were eating hay from their raised feeding platforms and on to the elephant island. Although I have always delighted in zoos, I was having a difficult time getting beyond the sadness that had settled within me.

I could not go to Samson, resurrecting the spirit of Dian Fossey, and offer him my soul. Too much stood between us . . . too much concrete and steel, too many owner's rights, too much conditioning of both of us. There was too much space, and its only erosion would remain limited to the embryonic messages sent by eyes seeing only fragments of the same world.

I was unable to bridge the gap between Samson and me, but Dian Fossey, Jane Goodall, and Birute Galdikas found a way to enter the world of the great apes.

These women, as Sy Montgomery explains in *Walking with the Great Apes,* made the pilgrimage into the animals' universe, not only to probe and record but to enter and join. Montgomery relates how each woman became a nurturer of individual animals, a scientific investigator, and a defender of the species against threats from their enemies, especially the human ones.

With most studies of wild animals, the human writes the contract. The researcher generally observes the animals from a distance or else drugs them, equips them with radio transmitters, and follows them with tracking devices. The relationship between human and animal is forced upon them. But that between Jane Goodall and the chimpanzees of Gombe, between Dian Fossey and the mountain gorillas she studied, and between Birute Galdikas and the wild orangutans of Tanjung Puting is different. These relationships formed on the animals' terms.

Dian Fossey, an American, Jane Goodall, an Englishwoman, and Birute Galdikas, a Canadian, are believed to have collected more scientific data on gorillas, chimpanzees, and orangutans than anyone else. They have been popularized in best-selling books, television documentaries, and a Hollywood motion picture. All three of these pioneers were protegees of the great Anglo-African archeologist Louis Leakey. World-famous by the time he died in 1972, Leakey through his spectacular fossil finds established Africa as the birthplace of mankind and proved that the ancestral line leading to humanity was very long. It was not until late in his career that he envisioned studies of the great apes. He was fifty-seven when he sent Jane Goodall into the field, sixty-three when he secured funding for Dian Fossey, and sixty-six when he chose Birute Galdikas to head up his orangutan study. Goodall was a former waitress and secretary, Fossey an occupational therapist who had flunked out of veterinary school, and Galdikas a graduate student in anthropology. But somehow Leakey knew that out of all those he could have chosen, these women would write a new chapter in the history of human-animal relationships.

Montgomery explains: "Some scientists who specialize in animal behavior believe one should not be emotionally involved with one's study subjects. But the relationship that these women dared share with the apes was the crucible in which their achievements were formed: the relationships informed their science, inspired their commitment, and transformed their lives. It is through their relationships with these animals that the women have transformed our views of ape and human, of animal and man."

Jane Goodall's great love of animals started when she was eighteen months old and her mother gave her a stuffed chimpanzee, which she named Jubilee and still owns. At the age of two her mother discovered earthworms in her bed; at four Jane watched a chicken for hours trying to discover how eggs were laid.

While still quite young, Goodall determined that she would go to Africa to study wild animals, despite the scoffing of teachers and the protests of some family members. But, Goodall explained, her mother, Vanna, "brought us up to never take no for an answer."

Despite the lack of a Ph.D., Goodall's insistence on studying animals won for her a membership on the team of Louis and Mary Leakey when they went to Olduvai in 1957 on a dig. Handling the fossils of prehistoric creatures and searching for the links that would tie them to man, Goodall realized the importance of Dr. Leakey's quest. He told her about the chimpanzees of Gombe, several hundred miles to the west. These creatures, Leakey explained, were large-brained, agile-handed primates, animals so like humans that early explorers had described them as human. A group of these animals lived by the shores of Lake Tanganyika in much the same environment that primitive people had enjoyed at Olduvai two million years ago.

Goodall arrived there in the summer of 1960 accompanied by her mother (who stayed for five months), a game ranger, and an African helper. It was the beginning of an adventure that continues to this day.

Soon after her arrival in Gombe, Goodall found herself a mentor in a seasoned female chimpanzee she named Flo, in whom she found the wizened old wise woman; Jane was her initiate. To Jane, as to no other human, Flo would pass on her experience of sexuality, motherhood, and the wisdom that comes with maturity, Montgomery says.

Early explorers depicted chimpanzees as violent brutes. The journals talked about their murderous rages and maniacal screams. "These monkeys have an ugly face," a seventeenth century text reads. "They are very wicked and bold . . . so bold that they attack man."

But watching the chimps from her perch, Goodall was impressed by their gestures of gentle affection. Chimps can be terrifying animals when aroused. A male chimp stands only four feet high but weighs around a hundred pounds and is stronger than two men. Yet Goodall found male chimps to be very considerate of one another. And after two chimps fought, almost invariably one would return to embrace his opponent, to lay an arm on the victor's back, to offer a hand to be kissed. As she noted in her book *In the Shadow of Man,* chimpanzees are very like humans both intellectually and emotionally.

Goodall discovered that the "maniacal screams" reported by less familiar observers were discovered by Goodall to be hoots of pleasure, heralding, for instance, the discovery of a tree laden with fruit. Sometimes in their excitement the chimps would hug one another as if in joyful congratulations.

In the chimpanzees Goodall saw the beginnings of what would make people define themselves as human, those characteristics we hold precious about ourselves: our imagination and playfulness and our connections to one another, forged by touch.

Because of her unique approach to communication with the chimpanzees, Goodall's studies are personal to the chimps and to her relationship with them. They have taught us much about infant development, family relationship, aggression, dominance, and sex.

Dian Fossey's introduction to Louis Leakey, the man who was the key to her career, as he had been for Jane Goodall, was something less than inspiring. She had saved her money to go on an African safari in 1963 and had traveled to the Leakey digs at Olduvai. But Leakey dismissed her as "another bothersome tourist": she broke a precious fossil in a fall, and then, nauseated by the pain of her sprained ankle, vomited on the fossil. But the depth of her dedication could hardly have been overlooked. After Mary Leakey wrapped Dian's sprained ankle, she insisted upon leaving the excavation site to climb up a 10,000-foot volcano in search of mountain gorillas. Three years later, Leakey had secured funding for her study.

Fossey's great need for solitude germinated during her childhood when she was a lonely only child living in a dysfunctional family. She always felt compelled to protect the vulnerable and the innocent. Dian wanted to become a veterinarian, but when she failed physics and chemistry she switched to occupational therapy and worked for a decade with disabled children.

Life never became easy for Fossey. She had to abandon her first research station in Zaire because of a political uprising. When she established Karisoke—named for the nearby volcanoes, Karisimbi and Visoke—she constantly fought the peaks, the jungle, dangerous beasts, snakes and insects, the wildlife poachers, and even the foundations that supported her.

Fossey believed strongly that she could not rush her contact with the gorillas, that she would need to allow the animals to become aware of her and comfortable with her presence from a distance. Then, with time and patience, she could move closer until they would finally allow her to be in their immediate presence. As the months moved into years, her funders urged her to speed up, but Fossey was not to be hurried. Slowly, over the months, she began to announce her presence. She uttered the animals' contentment sounds, she crunched on wild celery stalks as did they, and she scratched herself loud and long.

A little over two years from the start of her study, Fossey made physical contact. Peanuts, a young male, was the first gorilla to touch his fingers to hers. "Dian was lying on her back among the foliage, her right arm outstretched, palm up," Montgomery explains. "Peanuts looked at her intently; then he stood, extended his hand, and touched her fingers for an instant. *National Geographic* photographer Bob Campbell snapped the shutter only a moment afterward."

Peanuts pounded his chest with excitement and ran off to rejoin the other gorillas. With his touch, Peanuts had opened his family to her. Soon afterward the gorillas came forward and welcomed her into their midst. Fossey told a New York crowd gathered for a slide lecture in 1982 how the gorilla mothers let her hold their infants and how the silverbacks (mature gorillas) would groom her, parting her long dark hair with fingers as thick as bananas, yet deft as a seamstress's touch. "I can't tell you how rewarding it is to be with them," she said. "Their trust, the cohesiveness, the tranquility," and with her voice breaking she added, "It is really something."

A young male member of this gorilla family became particularly fond of Fossey and she of him. Whenever she was in the field, Digit, as she called him, always came to her and invited play by flopping on his back and kicking his feet in the air. Montgomery relates that in 1972 Campbell filmed "what is arguably one of the most moving contacts between two species on record." Although still a youngster in this film, Digit is huge, his head twice the size of Fossey's and his hands the size of dinner plates. He comes to her and with his enormous black hands gently takes her notebook, then her pen, and softly lays them in the foliage, then he rolls over to snooze at Fossey's side.

In her book, *Gorillas in the Mist*, Fossey tells how on one occasion she spotted the group across a ravine but, having been ill, she was not strong enough to cross it. "Uncle Bert," named after her favorite uncle, spotted her and led the entire group back across the ravine in order to be with her. Then Digit, who had been at the back of the group, "finally came right to me and gently touched my hair. . . . I wish I could have given them all something in return."

Digit and Fossey played together like children. He would strut toward her, playfully whacking at the foliage. She would tickle him, and he would chuckle and wrap his arms around her head. In a letter she wrote to a friend, Fossey said that Digit was fond of any object she happened to have with her. On one occasion she brought a candy bar and accidentally dropped it into a hollow tree stump. She asked Digit to retrieve it for her. "And according to script," Fossey wrote, "Digit reached one long, hairy arm into the hole and retrieved the candy bar. After one sniff he literally threw it back into the hole. The so-called 'wild gorillas' are really very discriminating in their tastes!"

Scientist Ian Redmond observed: "Dian's relationship with the gorillas is really the highest form of human-animal relationship. With almost any other human-animal relationship, that involves feeding the animals or restraining the animals or putting them in an enclosure, or if you help an injured animal—you do something to the animal. Whereas Dian and the gorillas were on completely equal terms. It was nothing other than the desire to be together. And that's as pure as you can get."

Fossey's continuing battle against poachers who killed gorillas to market their heads and hands escalated when her assistants found Digit's decapitated body. Serving as a sentry for his group, he sustained five spear wounds, held off six poachers and their dogs, and even managed to kill one of the poachers before dying. In his memory Fossey established the Digit Fund. Its purpose is to raise funds to protect the mountain gorillas. But Fossey herself was not to escape the enemy; in 1985 she was found murdered in her cabin by machete blows.

Fossey's death was not entirely in vain, for as Cal Fussman explains in Life magazine, "Today, gorilla hands are no longer used as ashtrays. Today, a zoo would risk public scorn if it acquired one of the world's 300 mountain gorillas. . . . Today, it is said that poachers, setting snares for antelope, chase gorillas out of the area for fear one might accidently sever a hand and die, for fear they might be blamed and jailed for five years. Today, the Digit Fund publishes an eight-page newsletter and solicits contributions from around the globe to continue research and help ensure the survival of the gorillas. . . ."

Birute Galdikas was the third member of Louis Leakey's "Trimate," as they were called. She spoke to Leakey for the first time after hearing him lecture at the University of California at Los Angeles, where she was pursuing a master's degree in anthropology. "Dr. Leakey looked at me very coldly and didn't say much. I could have been telling him he had dandruff for all his interest," she recalls.

But when she told him that she had already started with the arrangements for her study by contacting orangutan researchers in Sarawak, that got his attention. "I only support people who know what they want to do and are determined to do it," she recalls Leakey stating.

Galdikas knew exactly what she wanted to do. While still an undergraduate she had decided she wanted to study the wild orangutans in Indonesia, the apes with the human eyes. But even when Leakey decided that he would support her, adequate funding didn't materialize, and he suggested instead that she study pigmy chimpanzees in Zaire. That idea wasn't acceptable to Galdikas; she knew where she was going.

With only enough funds to buy four sets of clothing, notebooks, compasses, cooking and scientific gear, and a single flashlight, Galdikas and her husband, Rod Brindamour, set out for Indonesia on an adventure in which other scientists had for the most part failed. Past

studies of orangutans had been terminated with only incidental first-hand observation of orangutans. When they
reached their destination, the head of Indonesian parks
and nature reserves suggested that instead of their conducting their study in the well-mapped park in Sumatra,
she go where she wasn't following "in other people's footsteps." He recommended Tanjung Puting, a peninsula on
the south coast of Borneo, whose boundaries had never
been mapped and its interior never explored. Orangutans
had reportedly been seen there, he said.

The couple lived in poverty, eating mainly rice, tinned
sardines, and bananas. They cooked on an open fire;
their shoes and clothes rotted; they waded through deep
swamps, hacked their way through jungle vines with
machetes, and struggled to survive the poisonous insects,
crocodiles, fire ants, and snakes, including cobras, which
lurked everywhere in the camouflage of the jungle. In
spite of these efforts, it was two months before Galdikas
was to catch more than a glimpse of an orangutan.

Despite the danger, the wounds, disease, fatigue, and
disappointments, Galdikas—born in Germany, raised in
Canada, and educated in the United States—had found
home. For her, it has remained that for twenty-two years.

Patience and endurance eventually rewarded her: she
was able to track and maintain contact with individual
orangutans. Montgomery explains that orangutans, who
are fruit gatherers and constantly on the move, do not
travel in groups, as do chimpanzees and gorillas; adults
travel alone, except for dependent young. "They are soli-
tary, serene in their aloneness." For Galdikas, this
lifestyle meant that she had to gain separate acceptance
by each orangutan she studied.

Another phase of her study, however, evolved within months of the couple's arrival. Galdikas and her husband began to use their camp as a rehabilitation center for the captive orangutan orphans confiscated by the Indonesian government. From that time on the couple shared their bed with up to five clinging, biting, screaming infant orangutans at a time. While she still continued to study wild orangutans, over the years she mothered dozens of orphaned ex-captives. "Sometimes," Galdikas wrote in 1980, "I felt as though I were surrounded by wild, unruly children in orange suits who had not yet learned their manners." It was not unusual for her to trudge off to the swamp forest to study the wild orangutans with an infant orangutan clinging to her side.

"To have an orangutan choose your company is an honor few humans can imagine," Montgomery states in her book. She tells the story of one of Galdikas's female students and a visiting veterinarian getting caught in a rainstorm. "As they huddled beneath their shared raincape," Montgomery states, "Kusasi, a two-hundred-pound immature male ex-captive, and Tut, a large adult female, approached from the edge of the forest. Orangutans do not like rain; they are the only apes that make roofs over their treetop nests. The two orangutans lumbered over to the two women and ducked under the raincape. The four sat together silently, the orangutans' backs to the women's chests, for fifteen minutes, until the storm's end."

After Galdikas's work became famous as a result of *National Geographic* articles and television specials, American and European volunteers streamed into Camp Leakey, as she had named it. Earthwatch, an organization based in Watertown, Massachusetts, recruits laypeople who pay to assist with scientific projects, and the Orangutan Project is one of its most popular two- or three-week expeditions. Today, Earthwatch provides most of the funds for her work.

According to Montgomery, in recent years Western scientists' view of Galdikas's work has cooled behind complaints that she doesn't publish and provide information on her recent work. Some scientists question the value of information supplied by untrained volunteers, while others question the scientific value of her rehabilitation work with ex-captive orphans.

"But the bottom line," Montgomery states, "as with Jane and Dian, is that science is not her top priority. Science was the reason she first went into the field, but science is no longer what keeps her here." Direct relationships with the animals is.

Both science and self-involvement have played roles in the work of "Penny" Patterson, a California psychologist, who took on the task of teaching sign language to Koko, a female gorilla. Before her twelfth birthday, Koko had learned more than six hundred sign language words.

Patterson discovered that Koko had an affinity for pets and could care for animals other than members of her species. On her twelfth birthday, Patterson asked Koko what she wanted for her birthday. Immediately the gorilla drew her fingers across her cheeks, miming a set of whiskers, which was the sign for *cat*.

Earlier, Koko had named two of the household dogs, Apple and Smile, and various visiting cats: Candy, Golden Visitor, Surprise—and Stink, for a cat that had urinated in Patterson's closet.

With the request for the cat, Patterson gave Koko a small concrete statue of a cat. The gorilla kissed and rubbed the object against her cheek. Koko treated the item so gently that when a caretaker brought in three kittens abandoned by their Manx mother, she was immediately taken by the kittens. "Love that," Koko signed.

She picked up each one of the small kittens and blew gently in its face. After a time, Koko selected a small grey male, rocked it between her legs, and signed, "Koko love soft there," and two days later she named the tailless kitten "All Ball."

For six wonderful months Koko and All Ball played and cared for each other. Koko combed the kitten's hair, and when it purred so did the gorilla—the best way she could, in her deep, throaty voice.

But when All Ball was seven months old he was run over by a car. Koko received the news of the kitten's death in silence and then, according to reporter Anne Fadiman, she began to hoot the same soft distress cry she made when Patterson had left her for a night as an infant. For two months after the kitten's death the gorilla often cried to herself. When she was asked what she wanted for Christmas, Koko hesitantly signed, "Cat cat tiger cat." When Patterson brought Koko a yellow striped kitten, she was so excited "she spun around on her knuckles like a break dancer," Patterson reported.

The line separating humans from the apes may well he defined less by human measurement than by the limits of Western imagination, Montgomery suggests. "It may be less like a boundary between land and water and more like the lines we draw on maps separating the domains of nations."

We cannot measure animals by our own yardsticks. They are part of the world in their own way.

9

Plants Respond to Music, Prayer, and Humans

Plants thrive on Bach, jazz, and devotional music, and they wither when exposed to hard rock. This was the discovery a number of years ago of a professional singer turned scientist, and she opened a window to a wider view of a world in which all living things respond to the sound of music. With this finding, plants joined the ranks of humans and animals as sentient beings interacting with the aesthetic as well as the physical qualities of their environment.

Dorothy Retallack was a singer, wife of a medical doctor, a mother and stepmother of eight, and a fellow student of my friend Laurel Chivington. She was aware of my interest in organic gardening and in the electromagnetic factors influencing plant growth, so she was eager to tell me of her plant research. With what excitement did I learn of her promising results! Now, years later, I was elated to learn that she planned to resume her studies of the effects of music on plants.

We discussed her project on a Sunday after a social gathering at the Colorado Restorium. The visitors had moved on down Deer Creek Canyon Road, and in the lengthening shadows Retallack and I took the path from the lodge up past the chapel and sat down on the split-log benches at the edge of the Garden of Saint Francis.

Discussion had crowded the moments of the day, and it was comforting to sit in silence for a while, neither of us feeling an urgency to compete with the soft sounds of the wind passing by the ridges and sliding down the ravines.

A gust of wind caught the top of a large blue spruce nearby, and for a brief interlude it vibrated as though attuned to some song in the moving air. It was still bright with sunlight, although the shadows were beginning to climb its lower branches. I thought of the way it had served as a catalyst for so many of our experiences here, bringing the group together, sheltering us at times from more than rain or August sun. Its tree spirit was very real to us, filling the space around with an energy not found elsewhere, offering a contentment accepted but never defined.

I glanced at Retallack and discovered she was watching me. "You were a long way away," she said and smiled.

"Umm, not really," I responded, "Moments of silence seem to bring back memories. Anyway, the thought occurs to me—and who better to share it with than the 'Plant Lady'?—that we've always talked about the importance of these spruces to the Restorium, how they were the site of an Indian healing place, and how the great tree deva has remained to protect the sacredness of the grounds." She nodded but waited. "Well, under these trees people have come to play music and to sing for many years; before us, perhaps even the Indians did. Maybe this music was also important to the trees, perhaps helping them to become what they are today."

"Yes," she said, "Music is the breath and voice of nature—the sounds of the insects, birds, creatures calling to one another, flowers opening, the grass moving, the wind in the trees—and we try to add to these voices with our music. Can you fathom a world without music?"

"No," I said, "but we can't really hear each other's voices. We live in our own secluded worlds."

"I know," Dorothy said, "and that is one reason music is so important. It can be the link that helps bring us together."

Years before, we had sat in this same garden talking about her exciting discovery that plants are profoundly affected by the music in their environment. Her discovery was related to her profession. Retallack had been a professional mezzo soprano, but she retired from the stage when she married. As the children grew into adulthood, she once again started performing, but what she wanted more than anything was a college degree in music, so she enrolled at Temple Buell College. One requirement for her degree was a course in science, and for laboratory work in biology she decided to link science to music by monitoring the effects of music on plants.

Biology professor Francis F. Broman was unenthusiastic about her project, but he supported her nonetheless. Under his supervision, the experiments were conducted with rigid controls. Five varieties of plants—philodendrum,

radishes, corn, geraniums, and African violets—were planted from seed in plastic cups, with all variables equal. She
placed them in environment chambers in which light, temperature, and air were regulated automatically, and she
placed a loudspeaker in each of the chambers.

Retallack began her experiment by feeding the seeds
pure piano tones. One group received five minutes of the
key of B and D, followed by a five-minute rest interval,
for twelve hours each day. The second group was played
an F tone on the same schedule, and the third group was
fed an intermittent F tone for three hours.

The first and second group died within three weeks.
During their short life the seedling plants leaned as far
away from the loudspeakers as they could. The third
group survived and continued to grow.

For her second test, Retallack used petunia plants.
For one group she played rock music, the second group
semiclassical music and hymns, whith the volume being
the same for both groups. The control group produced
buds. By the end of two weeks the "rock music plants"
showed erratic growth and leaned away from the speaker. The second group flowered, and the plants leaned
toward the speaker. By the end of a month the rock
music plants were dead.

Two other music majors, Virginia Smith and
Marlene Maseberg, decided to replicate Retallack's
experiments. They planted squash in the control chambers, with one group exposed to rock music and the second group fed classical music. They conducted the
experiment for eight weeks, and by the end of this period
the plants in the rock chamber had grown away from the
speaker while the plants in the classical chamber had

wrapped themselves around the speaker. By the time Retallack conducted her next experiment some were suggesting that because she didn't like the rock music she was influencing the results. So she asked a stockroom clerk who knew nothing about the experiments to care for the plants and rewind the music tapes. The results were the same.

At this point the *Denver Post* started photographing the stages of change, including the use of time-lapse photography. The more press invited, of course, the more criticism ensued. When the critics wouldn't accept the explanation that the plants were trying to get as far away as possible from the percussive rock renditions of Led Zeppelin, Vanilla Fudge, and Jimi Hendrix, Retallack simply rotated the pots 180 degrees. The plants moved in the opposite direction.

In the tests that Retallack conducted during her next school year, she obtained the same results. Loud and dissonant sounds produced wilting and death. Soft sounds, classical music, and hymns enhanced growth and health in the plants. Climbing plants like morning glories, after being exposed to rock, not only couldn't crawl, they fainted in the opposite direction from the speakers. Cornstalks doubled over; beans were stunted and listed away from the speakers.

Trying to determine what it was about rock music that so jarred her plants, Retallack continued to wonder if it might be the percussive component in the music. She selected the Spanish tune "La Paloma," and played one version performed on steel drums to a chamber of plants and another version performed on strings to a second chamber. The percussion caused a slight lean from the vertical but nothing compared to rock music. The plants listening to the violin version leaned fifteen degrees toward the source of the music.

It has been said that silence is golden, but this proved to be the case in only one experiment. In all other investigations the seeds and plants bathed in pleasant sounds and devotional music outgrew the control group as well as the plants exposed to rock music. In one set of photos taken by the *Denver Post,* beans fed soothing music leaned into the speaker and had a rich upper growth, with strong, sturdy roots. Retallack told the *Post,* "The most fascinating thing is not the negative effect of rock music but the positive effect of soothing music. The control plants that grew in the quiet chambers were straight and healthy, but not as lush or as strong-rooted as the plants that got a little soft music every day for three weeks."

Retallack began to wonder how the effects of what she called "intellectual mathematically sophisticated music of both East and West" would influence plants. She chose choral preludes from Johann Sebastian Bach's "Orgelbüchlein" and the classical strains of the sitar played by Ravi Shankar, a Bengali musician.

"Listening" to Bach, the plants leaned an unprecedented thirty-five degrees toward the sounds of the prelude. But even this impressive result was shaded by the plants' reactions to Shankar. Straining to reach the source of the Indian music, they bent more than halfway to the horizontal.

Responding to the requests of many young people, Retallack followed her tests of Bach and Shankar with trials on country music. But the plants exposed to this music reacted similarly to the plants in the silent control chamber.

Jazz, on the other hand, produced an accelerated growth rate. The plants responded to the music of Duke Ellington and Louis Armstrong by leaning fifteen to twenty degrees toward the speaker, and their growth was greater than those of the silent chamber.

Retallack was inundated by mail and phone calls, including queries from scientists asking for copies of her published scientific papers. CBS television asked to set up a rock-versus-Shankar experiment for filming with time-lapse photography. She was anxious about the experiment but nevertheless confident that the results would be as expected. "This time the plants reacted even more than usual," related Retallack in her book, *The Sound of Music and Plants,* she tells of her meeting with Shankar and asking his opinion of the reason his music affected plants so favorably. He told her that he thought Bach, jazz, and his music had such profound effect on plants because all three were improvisational. All were in a sense religious. And all were created by musicians who really liked what they were doing. Shankar told her: "All three have love. I have this great love for what I play."

It was more than twenty years after all this that we sat talking in the Garden of Saint Francis, and I asked her, "Now you are working on another book. Why now, after all these years?"

She thought about my question for a few moments and then said, slowly, thoughtfully, "I feel there is a great need for the continuation of this research." She explained that following her studies and the publication of her book, serious articles claimed less attention than the sensationalized pieces appearing in the tabloid press. She received many letters and phone calls from persons intent on following up on her work, and although some of these contacts were from serious researchers, others came from "space cadets" convinced that Retallack had unlocked the secret to Jack and his beanstalk. A couple of music companies marketed recordings of "music to grow plants by."

"I expected some of these responses, and they didn't distress me, but what disappointed me was that so many members of the scientific community blew off the findings and suggested that other variables were the causes. They made these statements without carrying out their own research," Retallack told me. "With today's escalating problems not only with the environment but with our adolescents, whose bizarre behavior may be fed by television and their music, I believe it is important to take a more serious look at the way sound and music influence our lives. Because we are not separate from the world in which we live, one way to examine these effects is through plants. I hope my investigations will draw attention to these needs."

The interaction between plants and humans has also been demonstrated in the work of Dr. John Pierrakos, a New York psychiatrist. Clairvoyant all his life, he uses his perceptions of the human aura to assist him in his diagnoses.

Pierrakos explained that he usually sees three layers of energy around most of his patients. The first, a dark band no more than one-sixteenth to one-eighth of an inch thick, lies close to the skin and looks like a transparent crystalline structure. The second band, a broader dark blue layer reminiscent of a cluster of iron filings, forms an ovid envelope around the body when seen from the front. The third band is a lightish blue haze of radiant energy that extends, when the patient is in good health, several feet away from the body and accounts for the reason we sometimes describe happy persons as radiant.

The pyschiatrist noticed that when his patients were depressed, stressed, fearful, or just generally in a bad mood, his office plants sitting nearby reflected these negative states: the flowers appeared wilted, and the leaves drooped.

Familiar with the investigations of Backster, Retallack, and Pierrakos, inventor Dan Carlson took seriously the influence of sound and music on plants and has been demonstrating on a large scale the use of music to increase food production. He does this through a process he calls Sonic Bloom, a mixture of sound and nutrients that alledgedly makes plants grow in miraculous proportions.

Carlson, who heads up the Dan Carlson Scientific Enterprises of Blaine, Minnesota, states that he spent fifteen years in developing the sound/spray process. The key to greater yields, earlier maturity, and improved tastes, according to Carlson, is the use of a high-frequency electromagnetic wave developed through natural sounds. The wave's range is similar to the frequency range of many bird calls, such as those made by swallows, martins, and warblers. The sounds open the stomata, the tiny openings on the leaf surface, thus allowing a plant to more readily absorb nutrients. Carlson applies an organic foliar spray while the plants are exposed to the sound via loudspeakers.

One of the proponents of Carlson's system is Ken Taylor, owner of Windmill Point Farms and Nursery near Montreal. He conducted initial trials on carrots, soaking germinated carrot seeds in a nutrient solution, leaving them overnight with a cassette tape playing Carlson's high-frequency sound. Taylor claims the crop of carrots was the best he ever produced.

Taylor also treated a hundred citrus plants with Carlson's process, leaving them outside during the summer and into late fall, when they survived temperatures of 14 degrees Fahrenheit. When he examined them in December, the dark, glossy foliage of the grapefruit, orange, and lemon trees showed no blemishes.

Don Jansen of Fort Meyers, Florida, told *Acres, USA* magazine that he increased his cucumber count by 400 percent using Sonic Bloom. At LaBelle, Florida, Roy McClurg estimated at least a 30 percent yield increase in his orange crop using the process. Many other American gardeners and farmers have reported unusual yields with the sound.

In Israel, 450 endangered North African varieties of shrubs, fruit, and nut trees have been successfully treated by Carlson's system. It is now in use in fourteen countries and in all 50 states of the U.S.A.

A certain quality of the human voice also stimulates the health and growth of plants, not only in song but also through the encouragement and affirmation of prayer. This was successfully demonstrated by Reverend Franklin Loehr and 150 members of his congregation.

The discovery occurred in 1952 when the Reverend Loehr, pastor of the First Congregational Church in Los Angeles, learned of an experiment being conducted by Dr. J. B. Rhine at Duke University to determine whether prayer could affect the growth of plants. Interestingly enough, while Rhine's results were never considered significant, the Reverend Loehr's finding created quite a stir both in the scientific community and with religious groups, and it led to Loehr's writing a best-selling book, *The Power of Prayer on Plants*.

At the time that his imagination was fired by Dr.

Rhine's work, Loehr had already established the Religious Research Foundation and for more than two years had been conducting a prayer circle.

For his first experiment Loehr and his researchers purchased six tin bread pans, some lima beans, sweet pea seeds, corn kernels, and two bottles of spring water. One bottle would be held by the prayer circle and prayed over; it would be marked Aquator. The other bottle would be used as a control and would not receive prayer. The Aquator was given individual prayer as it passed from one person to another. That bottle was then placed in the center of the group while the church members prayed collectively that it would give the plants health and greater growth.

The researchers filled the six pans with dirt dug outside the church. In two of the pans they placed eight kernels of corn each; in two pans they planted eight lima beans; and in the final pair they set eight sweet pea seeds. All pans received the same amount of water, but only half the pans received the Aquator.

A week later, three corn seedlings appeared in the pans with the treated water while none appeared in the control pans. The following week four more seedlings appeared in the treated pans, for a total of seven, and three seedlings showed in the control pans. The lima beans had a difficult time breaking through the hard clay soil, but four beans managed to sprout and grow in the treated pans while none made it through in the untreated pans. The researchers found less difference between the two sweet pea pans, but even so, the plants in the treated pans outnumbered the controls three to two.

Reasoning that if positive prayer produced growth,

then negative prayer would inhibit growth, Loehr designed a study to test his theory. A member of his prayer circle, Erwin Prust, agreed to play the villain. Loehr cut ivy slips and put them in two pots. One pot received prayers for growth, and the other was exposed Prust's prayer for non-growth. In the beginning the researchers found no measurable difference between the growth of the ivy in the two pots, but two weeks later the growth-prayer plants were thriving while the other plants were dead.

Loehr established rigid controls with Prust for the next experiment. To prevent the possibility of "choice," Loehr told Prust to rest a forearm on the table and point a finger toward the edge of a cake pan in which twenty-three corn kernels had been planted on each side of the divider. Loehr spun the pan, and when it stopped, the side by Prust's finger was marked for receiving prayers. During the eight days of the experiment Loehr kept the pan sealed while Prust delivered his positive prayers to one side and negative prayers to the other side. At the end of the eight days, Loehr removed the paper seal and found sixteen healthy seedlings on the positive side and only one seedling on the negative side.

During the year, Loehr and his prayerful experimenters took thousands of measurements on dozens of experiments in which they tested many variables. These included different types of prayers as well as prayers done individually and collectively. They produced the most effective results when, rather than using a group prayer, the members of the group prayed individually in the manner each felt to be the most comfortable. Using this approach, prayed-over corn outgrew the non-prayed-over corn on an average of 26 percent, and the prayed-over wheat outgrew the non-prayed-over wheat by 27 percent.

With a grant of $1,000 for their prayer experiments from the Parapsychology Foundation in New York City, the Reverend Loehr's researchers established a program in which the participants in the prayer circle received home experiment kits. In order to confirm "prayer power," the kits contained cotton instead of soil, since cotton would reduce nutrient variable from outside the seed itself to near zero.

The prayer group sent test results for tabulation and analysis to Mabel Sones of Cedar Rapids, Iowa, who had worked with Dr. Rhine on prayer-plant research. In the first class her report showed a 30.6 percent overall prayer advantage, with twelve of the thirteen experimenters getting a net positive results. Out of the 28 prayer experiments, 21 produced an advantage of positive growth for prayed-over plants.

The Reverend Loehr's findings over a three-year period, in which more than 150 persons performed more than 700 experiments using more than 27,000 seeds and seedlings and taking more than 100,000 measurements, indicated that four our of six people could get from 15 to 50 percent increase in growth with seedlings that received positive prayer against those that did not receive prayer. As well, about one person in six obtained a steady reverse result in growth with seedlings. Out of the 150 persons tested, the researchers found that three or four members of the group were so positive, strong, and concentrated in prayer that they were capable of retarding growth, even on occasion killing seedlings that had sprouted and plants that were growing.

What emerges as the most important in the work of Retallack, Pierrakos, Carlson, and Loehr is the evidence that plants can interact with humans for the mutual benefit of both.

Humans have always known, of course, that their lives depended on plants, for without plants their food would be nonexistent. And from ancient times people have used plant offerings for everything from medicines and cloth to building materials. Their aesthetic qualities have enriched our lives; in fact, life as we know it would without plants be impossible.

Yet the pioneering investigations of the visionaries who worked with plants and those discussed earlier in the book reveal a new world of interspecies communication in which the isolation of the kingdoms of nature need no longer be accepted. With the establishment of mediums of communication between man and plant through music, sound, thoughts, and emotions, the sharing of a new level of understanding of a world in which all life is one is no longer an impossible dream.

10

Human-Animal Communication
after Death

In our culture there is a general assumption that only humans are blessed with souls and immortal life, that once an animal's brief span is spent on earth it is gone forever except as its memory lingers on in the hearts of those who loved it.

It has also been said that only humans are aware of their death, and that this awareness proves that only humans have immortal souls. We harbor the thought that only *we* cling to life as a precious commodity. Most people do not entertain the idea that other animals experience anxiety or fear of death; we imagine that, since they do not comprehend that life will end, death has no meaning to them.

But there is a great deal of evidence that many species, at least, are definitely aware of death. Dogs, chimpanzees, elephants, cats, wolves, and dolphins, to name only a few, often show great stress and obvious mourning at the loss of a companion. As a matter of fact, the grief exhibited by a creature at the death of a companion from a *different* species is one of the most graphic demonstrations of the reality of interspecies communication and the kind of bonding that can take place between members of separate species.

A woman wrote to me that her dog stopped eating and eventually died of depression when its longtime companion, a parakeet, died. Another woman's cat grew extremely depressed following the death of the family dog. A Skye Terrier called Greyfriars Bobby has become famous for keeping a daily vigil at the grave of his master in Edinburgh. Koko mourned for days after her kitten All Ball was killed by a truck.

An awareness of death and the seeming active pursuit of this state, because of grief and despair, is found in the story of Tom, a seven-year-old collie that belonged to Harold Myers of Houston, Texas. Harold and Tom were inseparable, and it was understandable that the dog was lost without his master when Harold left home to join the armed forces during the Vietnam War. But, although Tom was unhappy with Harold's absence and moped a great deal alone, he seemed to accept the separation with resigned patience.

From the day Harold was killed in action (several days before the Myers family was notified), Tom exhibited a determination to end his own life. Three blocks from the Myers home was a railroad track. Tom stretched himself across the track, but before a train arrived two men spotted him from the crossing and pulled him from the rail. But the following day the big collie stayed on the track until the train came. Did he somehow believe that he would once again be with his master?

Tom's apparent suicide poses some interesting questions. If he had been killed on the first attempt, one could argue that the dog just happened to be on the track at the wrong time. Yet he was saved once, only to return. And if death was not his intention, he could very easily have moved out of the way. What understanding of life and death did Tom possess? He understood them clearly enough to choose one over the other.

What does a knowledge of death imply? If a creature is aware that the occurrence of death eliminates mortal life, it suggests that this creature can project into the minutes, hours, or days ahead with the knowledge that the lost one will not return. There is the determination, however arrived at, that an irreversible change has taken place.

When I was a boy growing up on a Kansas farm, we had a neighbor, T.J. Randle, who raised horses. He understood the working of those horses the way some people today understand computers. He could gentle-break tough customers better than anyone I have ever known. Everyone in the area recognized this feat, and people would say, "Ol' T.J. must be part horse himself; he understands them, and they seem to understand him."

T.J. allowed his horses to graze around his house. At the entrance to his drive was a gate that had to be opened and shut when driving in and out of his place. When he died and the ambulance came to pick up his body, all of his horses were standing quietly around the house, but when the ambulance bearing T.J.'s body exited through the gate, the horses also stampeded through it and headed up the road with the ambulance. Not wanting to hit one of them, the driver drove slow. He stopped once to ask a neighbor following behind in his car if something should be done about the horses. "Naw," the neighbor said. "They'll get tired pretty soon and go back. "They didn't. They galloped the five miles to town and surrounded the ambulance while T.J.'s body was being moved inside the funeral home.

Someone phoned the sheriff, who said he would get some deputies to round them up before they caused an accident. But he needn't have bothered, for when they were next spotted they were already on the road leading back to the ranch.

An understanding of life and death and what it would take to keep the one from becoming the other was demonstrated a number of years by a dog in Ohio. One day in 1979, Rae Anne Knitter and Ray Thomas were hiking near Cleveland, Ohio, when Ray stepped out on a shale ledge to take a picture. The ledge gave way, and Ray fell eighty feet to the hard ground below. His body stopped, however, on the edge of a small stream, and he lay face down in the water.

Rae Anne's mongrel dog Woodie immediately broke loose from her leash and ran to the edge of the cliff. A moment later she, too, plunged to the rocks below. Somehow, she seemed to realize there was no time for other options. Woodie broke both hips in the fall but managed to drag herself by her front paws to Ray's side and nuzzle his head out of the water.

When Rae Anne arrived at the scene, Woodie was keeping Ray's head out of the water, and he regained consciousness long enough to tell his fiancé, "I'm broken all over."

Rae Anne tried to put her hand under Ray's head, but Woodie pushed her away. The girl summoned help, and rescuers carried Thomas to an ambulance. It was also necessary to carry Woodie, for she could no longer move.

Thomas spent nearly three months in intensive care from a torn spinal cord, three broken vertebrae, and a broken left elbow and right wrist. But he acknowledged that "if it wasn't for Woodie, I'd be dead." As for Woodie, in addition to the broken hips, she sustained fractures of seven toes, and it took three months to recover from her life-saving leap. For her heroics Woodie was named the 1980 Ken-L Ration Dog Hero of the Year. She was awarded a gold medal, a gold-plated leash and collar, a one-thousand-dollar bond, and a pastry dog-house filled with dog food.

How many of us would have the courage to perform Woodie's feat? She must have known the extent of the risk. Dogs do not jump from heights their bodies can't handle; instinct or some inner knowing provides this caution. Yet Woodie, with only a second's calculation, plunged to the ground below. Even then, badly broken, she managed to drag herself to Ray's side and raise his head out of the water.

There are myriad stories of animals risking their lives to save a member of their family or their herd. Cynthia Moss, director of the Amboseli Elephant Research Project in Kenya, has spent more than a decade studying elephants and tells what happened when hunters attacked one of the groups she was studying. A young female elephant that Moss called Tina was shot in the chest, and the bullet penetrated her lung. The herd took flight, but as the groaning young elephant, with blood pouring from her mouth, was about to slip to the ground, her mother, Teresia, and Trista, another older female, positioned themselves on each side of Tina in order to hold her upright. But their efforts failed, and Tina collapsed and died.

Teresia and Trista tried to resuscitate Tina and raise her. Tina's mother tried to lift the limp body from the ground with her great tusks, snapping off one of the tusks in the attempt. When the elephants finally accepted Tina's death, they refused to leave the body. They dug in the rocky dirt with their trunks and sprinkled soil over Tina's body. Some brought back branches and laid them over the body. Throughout the night the members of Tina's family stood vigil over their fallen kin. None left until dawn, and Tina's mother was the last to leave.

Dolphins and whales have been observed supporting injured companions above the water in order to let them breathe, and wolves will bring food to injured members of the pack. Michael W. Fox, a veterinarian, wrote that once in India he saw a male dog tenderly licking the sores on the face of a sick female dog and snapping at the flies around her to keep them away. "When I gave the pair some bread," he said, "because they were obviously starving, the male let his companion have her fill first."

If love is the highest expression of the soul, as all religions claim, it doesn't seem reasonable to credit the human with a soul because of these qualities and to withhold it from another animal who has demonstrated self-sacrificing love for another being. Dr. Fox stated in an article: "Such altruism can only stem from empathy—the ability to put oneself in another's place—and surely that is a sign that animals have souls."

Animals have emotional lives. They experience love, grief, fear, and joy. If these attributes cannot be assigned to the soul, where would we assign them? They care not only for their own kind but for other species as well. These qualities are not limited to the human species, so why would we imagine the soul and the spiritual dimensions of life to be the exclusive property of the human animal? Gary Kowalski, a graduate of Harvard Divinity School, a Unitarian Universalist minister, and author of *The Souls of Animals*, states: "To me, animals have all the traits indicative of soul. For soul is not something we can see or measure. We can only observe its outward manifestations: in tears and laughter, in courage and heroism, in generosity and forgiveness. . . . "

The existence of a soul assumes an essence or quality of beingness not to be found within the physical properties of an individual life, nor is it one that ceases to exist upon the death of the physical vehicle. As soul is generally understood, it implies continued existence of awareness after physical death.

The case for the immortality of animals is strengthened by the experiences of persons who have had deceased pets return to them during life-and-death situations, experiences that can hardly be discounted as hallucinations or flights of the imagination. It would be difficult to persuade Robin Deland, for instance, that his deceased dog didn't return in order to save his life.

In the Colorado mountains several years ago, Deland was driving at night on an unpaved, narrow, and winding road near Gunnison. He had started up a sharp incline when suddenly, only a short distance ahead in the road, a dog appeared in his headlights. The animal stood there unmoving, and Deland had to brake to a stop. He sat frozen in his seat, for the dog, now only a few feet away and clearly detailed by his car lights, was his collie Jeff. Why was he so sure? Maybe only those who have had a pet as a constant companion for a dozen years can understand. Deland had found the young collie dying alongside a highway after having been struck by a vehicle. He rushed the dog to an animal hospital, and after the collie underwent extensive surgery, he nurtured the dog back to health. They were extremely close. Deland knew every hair on the dog's body. And Jeff was extremely large for his breed. He had a massive head but a somewhat short nose for a collie. Deland is quite certain that his rendezvous on a rocky mountain precipice was with Jeff even though the dog had died six months earlier.

Deland was so awed and bewildered by the dog's presence that he doesn't remember getting out of his car. He recalls walking toward the dog, and he believes that he held out his hand and called Jeff's name. Almost within reach, the animal suddenly whirled away and walked slowly up the road toward the peak of the incline. Deland followed, trying to catch up with Jeff, trying to get close enough to touch him. He topped the incline, but just beyond, silhouetted by the moonlight, was a massive rock slide, burying the road. If his car had reached that point, the effect on Deland would have been certain death. There was no way he could have kept from plunging off the cliff in a drop of several hundred feet.

Deland told me that he doesn't know how long he stood on the edge of the precipice, staring at the rock slide and then to the depths below. He imagines that he might have been in some kind of trance, unable for several minutes to cope with the impact of the event. Shaking himself out of the spell, he remembers, he immediately looked around for Jeff and called out to him. But the dog had disappeared as mysteriously as he had suddenly come back into Deland's life.

Deland doesn't have witnesses to back up his story. But for him, no other witness is necessary. Several witnesses can attest to the occurrences that pulled the Raymond Peters family from a certain death trap one December night.

Raymond and his wife Suzanne had turned in early, for they were exhausted. One of their children, who had an upset stomach, had kept them up the night before. And the two nights before that they had worked into the wee hours on their income taxes. Bed was a welcome haven, and they were almost asleep by the time they stretched out. But their sleep that night was fated to be even shorter.

About four hours after retiring, both Raymond and Suzanne were awakened by a dog barking. Raymond recalls that, still half-asleep, he called out to his Scottie, Mac, to hush, and he remembers his wife saying, "What in the world is the matter with him?" But Mac was not to be ignored. Raymond explained that there wasn't any way they could fall back asleep, for the next instant, Mac was barking frantically almost in his ear. Raymond sat up, saying, "Damn it, Mac, . . ." thinking the dog wanted to go outside to urinate. But then he smelled the smoke. Instantly wide awake, he leaped out of bed. Their bedroom door was closed, and when they opened it, choking smoke had already filled the hallway. They could feel the heat of the fire in the ceiling, and the far end of the hall was aflame, but it had not yet reached the children's bedroom.

They grabbed the still-sleeping youngsters in their arms and fled from the house. Minutes later, the old dwelling was engulfed in flames. The fire department had already been called by a neighbor, who had been awakened not by seeing and smelling the fire but by the barking dog. The sound was so close, he said, that he first thought the dog was inside his own home. He then looked out the window for the dog and saw the flames. By the time the firemen arrived, the house was too far gone to save, and they concentrated on keeping the fire from spreading. Raymond and Suzanne Peters lost all of their possessions, but their children survived.

Only when their neighbor said to them, "My God, you would never have made it if it hadn't been for your dog. I didn't know that you had gotten another dog after Mac died. . . . Where is he, Ray? Did he get out of the house?"

The Peterses looked at each other, speechless for several moments. Raymond is not sure what he said at this point, but he recalls that it felt as though his heart had stopped, and he was dizzy. He heard Suzanne say, "Raymond—oh, Raymond," as though frightened, and then himself saying, "It was Mac. . . . I know Mac's bark. . . . We've never had any other dog." No need to look for the Scottie, for he had made his exit from life three months previously.

My own experience of this nature happened with a dachshund we had raised from a pup and had for thirteen years. Many kinds of animals have enriched my life, but I doubt that I would be writing this chapter if my experience with the dachshund, Phagen, had not occurred. It made great demands on me, and I am grateful for this.

Late one night I was awakened from a deep sleep by Phagen's persistent barking. I listened for a few moments, hoping he would stop and I wouldn't have to go outside and scold him. The barking continued, sharp and quite insistent, so I pulled on some clothes and made my way to his pen. He was not outside his doghouse, so I looked inside with my flashlight, and there he lay. He had been dead for several hours, as the body was frozen stiff. I lay awake for some time, puzzled as to how I could hear Phagen barking so clearly when he had been dead for several hours.

But Phagen was to bark again. For two consecutive nights at exactly the same hour, I heard him barking. Both nights I went outside. The first night I saw nothing but an empty pen and doghouse. But the second night as I approached his pen in the semi-darkness of a waning moon, I saw him in the shadows, waiting, and as I drew closer I saw him wag his tail. Awed, bewildered, I reached toward him . . . but in that moment he was gone. He never barked again. Since then, I have asked myself many times if Phagen came back for a final farewell. I might wonder whether I was experiencing an extremely vivid dream or was having hallucinations, and this might be plausible except that my neighbor, who was unaware that Phagen had died, asked me the morning after my final experience if something was wrong with Phagen because he had barked so much on the two previous nights.

In his book, *The Evidence for Life after Death*, Martin Ebon tells the story of a cocker spaniel named Ronnie who died while undergoing an operation. Ronnie's mistress was sitting beside her phone at her home waiting for the operation's results when she heard the sound of his dog tags tinkling and his claws clattering across the porch, but when she held open the door, nothing was there. "She knew her old friend had died and returned home for the last time," Ebon said.

According to Native American traditions, the spirit lives on after the death of its body. "All forms of life are sacred. Everything that lives is an expression of the Great Spirit," O-She-Na, an Indian medicine woman, told me after a meeting at the Indian Center in Wichita, Kansas. "As part of this All That Is, anything brought into existence remains in existence, forever—as I understand time—moving toward an understanding of the life force, the Great Spirit."

This philosophy is in keeping with the teachings of Socrates, who claimed that all animals are immortal and that the soul does not perish at the dissolution of the body. And the early school of Platonists claimed that the souls of all living creatures were a part of the universal soul of the world, and when the body died the soul would go to some other state.

Other thinkers expressed similar ideas. Solomon, in one of his despondent moods, ironically asked the question: "Who knoweth the spirit of man that goeth upward, and the spirit of a beast that goeth downward to the earth?" And he noted: "That which befalleth the sons of men befalleth beasts; as the one dieth so dieth the other; yea, they have all one breath; so that a man hath no preeminence above a beast. All go to one place."

Seventeenth-century theologian John Wesley,

founder of the Methodist Church, while speaking of a general restoration of all animal life, declared that "the animals shall be delivered from the bondage of corruption into glorious liberty, even a measure, according as they are capable, of the liberty of the children of God. . . ." Then he asked the questions: "What if it should then please the All-Wise and All-Gracious Creator to raise the creatures, which we now call inferior animals, to a higher grade in the scale of creation? What if it should please Him, in the great regeneration, when He makes us equal to the angels, to make them what we are now?" It's a sobering thought.

At times when pets have allegedly returned from the grave to visit their former owners their mission was not a life-saving one. Take Bobby, for instance, a black mongrel who wagged his tail with wild excitement, bounded toward the homecoming soldier who was his neighbor, and excitedly licked the young man's face. Nothing unusual about this typical greeting between a man and his dog after a long separation . . . except for the fact that the dog had been dead for nine months.

Bobby had been very fond of the young man who lived next door, and they had spent many hours playing and hiking together. Then the man left for the Army, and while he was away, Bobby died.

Parapsychological researcher Ian Currie, who tells the story, explains that the man did not know the dog had died, and he was delighted upon his return home to have Bobby bound excitedly to him.

"For several minutes, Bobby made a terrific fuss. Then he ran off into a batch of dahlias," Currie explained.

The following day, the young man was told of the

dog's death—and that its body had been buried in the dahlia bed.

The ex-soldier told Currie: "There is no question in my mind that I played with Bobby. I knew him so well there couldn't be any mistake."

Frank Talbert's life was saved by a visit from a neighbor's dog. On the night it happened he was profoundly but very contentedly tired. He stood looking out of his large picture window at the thunderstorm hovering over the mountains to the north. He mused that it would be a good night to sleep. A fire to chase the early October chill, a needed rain falling outside, peaceful solitude, what more could he ask for? he wondered.

Talbert had spent the day thinning some of the timber from his property near Breckenridge, Colorado. A successful real estate broker in Denver, Talbert had constructed a three-room cabin on ten acres of mountain land and enjoyed visiting his hideaway. Although he spent some weekends there with his family, he was particularly happy when he could get away by himself for a few days. On this occasion, he planned to spend a week and a half alone to work on the property.

He banked the fire for the night and went to bed. The wind started up, rain pelted down on the cedar roof, and occasional lightning allowed him a brief glimpse of the rock face east of the cabin. But Talbert drifted quickly into sleep. How long he slept he wasn't sure, but a sound awakened him. It was still raining, the lightning had drawn closer, and the thunder now came in rolling crashes and crescendos, but this was not the sound that jarred him awake. Somewhere outside a dog was barking. Talbert sat up in bed, listening. The bark came again, this time at some distance. He was starting to slide back down in the bed when the barking seemed but a few feet from his door. It was both a howl and a bark, and Talbert decided the dog was in some kind of trouble and was asking for help or perhaps simply wanted shelter from the storm.

He opened the door but could see only a few feet through the driving rain. He called, but there was no answer. Talbert was about to shut the door again when a flash of lightning provided him a glimpse of a dog not more than thirty feet away. He called to the animal, but instead of coming closer, the dog moved slowly away, giving a mournful, appealing howl while doing so. Obviously, Talbert decided, the dog wanted him to follow, and he wondered if she had puppies that were exposed to the storm. He quickly slipped on his boots and into a hooded parka. The dog was waiting for him. Talbert was able to get within a few feet of the dog before it turned away, evidently expecting him to follow. He had been close enough to see by his flashlight beam that the dog appeared to be a red setter, except that it had a white neck and chest.

But Talbert followed the dog only a few yards when everything around him turned red, and a tremendous explosion nearly deafened him. Lightning had struck his cabin, and a fire had started in his bedroom. He managed to haul some of his possessions outside, but in the rain and darkness, relieved only by the light from the fire and the headlights of his pickup truck, it was difficult work. Most of the cabin was destroyed, and there was little he could do except watch the flames from his truck.

Only when he was preparing to leave and drive to the nearest neighbor's place did Talbert remember the dog.

By this time the rain had stopped, the sky had partly cleared, and the moon provided some illumination. He looked for the setter, but the dog was not around. As he searched for the animal it dawned on Talbert that the lightning had struck the bedroom area, and the reason the fire burned so intensely was that his mattress and bedding must have ignited instantly. If the dog had not coaxed him outside, he would most likely have died in that bed.

When he told his story to his neighbor, the man was perplexed. "The dog you describe sounds like Sandy," the man said, slowly shaking his head. "She was a setter but with that very unusual marking of a white chest and neck. . . . "

"That must be her, all right. My God, where is she? I think I have to thank her for my life!" Talbert exclaimed.

The neighbor didn't say anything for several moments. He stared at Talbert and then slumped in his chair. His voice was hardly audible as he whispered, "That won't be possible, Frank. She died more than two months ago."

Sandy still physically alive when she lured Frank Talbert away from danger? No, no mistake about her death; she had been buried near her owner's home. Could it have been another setter? Possible, of course, but one with the same unusual markings as Sandy and living in the same area? The possibility was rather remote. Perhaps a dog from the same litter as Sandy? No, she was born in Texas and brought to Colorado when she was eight years old. Perhaps it was one of Sandy's pups with the same markings? Sandy never had a litter; an operation prevented this. So Talbert—and we—will never know. Yet Talbert will remember his visitor for a long time. His neighbor gave him a picture of Sandy. He framed it, and it sits on his desk in his home.

The experiencing of the continued existence of animals after their death has occurred to persons who have had out-of-body experiences. For a number of years when I served as a trainer at the Monroe Institute of Applied Sciences near Faber, Virginia, I participated in five or six week-long workshops each year on altered states of consciousness, and although the central purpose of the sessions was to help the attendees to get in touch with the hidden dimensions of themselves, the shifts in perception sometimes brought about an out-of-body experience. Once a young clinical psychologist from Cincinnati had a very vivid and moving experience of sharing with her deceased mother. In it she learned some things about her early life of which she was previously unaware. The physical survival of animals played only an incidental role in this emotional drama and probably would have been overlooked except for a question asked by a member of the group: "Did your mother seem content with what was happening to her on that plane?"

"Oh, yes," the woman responded. "She was peacefully happy, almost tranquil. She shares with her parents who are there, and one of her sisters, and there are friends. And, then, Penny was close by her side all of the time. She loved that little dog. . . ." The psychologist then resumed her account of the sharing between her and her mother, and no further mention was made of the dog. Her comments seemed an afterthought, but what was interesting to me was the complete acceptance of the animal's presence. It is also interesting to note that there were several persons in that group who allegedly had experiences on the astral plane, and not one expressed surprise that the woman's pet could be on that level.

During another Monroe workshop, a young electrical engineer from Duluth, Minnesota, was telling the group about his out-of-body experience when he happened to mention a deceased pet that entered the picture. "As I passed through a tunnel and emerged into this very bright light," he said, "I sensed that I was going to be able to see my brother again. He had died five years before. I felt his presence, and excitement was pounding through me. But quite suddenly, bounding happily toward me, was Racer, my brother's collie that had died shortly after he did. I loved that dog almost as much as my brother did, but I certainly didn't have any thoughts about seeing him again. Yet, there he was, jumping playfully on me and barking, just as he had always done when I had been away for a while. . . . Then he took off and I followed . . . and, yes, there ahead of us was my brother!"

Persons who have had out-of-body experiences as a result of clinical death will often relate that they view their ill or damaged bodies from a short distance and not infrequently watch while doctors struggle for their physical survival. Sometimes during this interim, while they are apart from their bodies, they will converse with known or unknown entities who are present. A woman, whom I'll call Barbara, told me that during a clinical death experience she found herself walking along a path in a meadow and saw, trotting alongside, her cat Lilly, who had died two years before. Suddenly feeling called back to the site of her body, she hurried back along the path, with Lilly running beside her. Then the cat stopped, as though knowing it could go no farther, Barbara said, and sat down in the path as though to wait.

Immortality devoid of individuality has no meaning beyond the perpetuation of a species. Regardless of how brilliant or stupid a human being is, we are likely to assume that these states have little application as regards his or her immortality. While we can easily accept that animals will sometimes demonstrate greater intelligence, sensitivity, awareness, and kindness than at least some human beings, we may deny them immortality simply because they belong to a different species. We do this in spite of arguing that the soul is not constructed of material substance; we seem to believe that the quality of "soulness" has something to do with the shape, form, and function of a physical body.

In the preceding pages I have cited animals of considerable intelligence, intuitiveness, insightful perception, and caring to the point of self-sacrifice for members of the same as well as other species. These qualities were expressed individually and not always in keeping with what we have come to expect of a member of that species. Are these unusual demonstrations expressions of creatures whose consciousness has outgrown that of the species in general? By the same reasoning, how do we compare the mental acuities of Einstein and Leonardo da Vinci with the rest of us? Further, how much individuality are we expressing when we are but a single integral of collective action? Is this something other than herd instinct?

The question then becomes: if we are unwilling to assign individual immortality to all life forms even when individuality is clearly there, what criteria would we use to assign immortality to some life forms and not to others? At what point does a creature gain immortality? When it has a grip on human language? Are dolphins withholding the blessing of immortality for us until we master dolphin language?

The man who carries both the distinction and the blame for the development of evolutionary theory, Charles Darwin, had the following to say in *The Descent of Man*: "We have seen that the senses and intuitions, the various emotions and faculties, such as love, memory, attention, curiosity, imitation, reason, etc., of which man boasts, may be found in an incipient or even sometimes in a well-developed condition in the lower animals." From what we know now, that may be an understatement.

It no longer seems reasonable to suppose that only one species, the human, is in a position to benefit from the struggles of living on this planet—the only creature that can learn from this experience and thereby move onward and upward, with all other species merely serving as props to the human drama. Having studied the evidence, we would more logically infer that there is one far-off divine event, as Tennyson put it, toward which the whole creation moves.

11

Transcending the Barriers to Interspecies Communication

Anyone who has truly bonded with a member of another species finds it difficult to relate to life, whatever its form, in the same way as before. The boundaries between oneself and another creature have become more diffused, less clearly defined; the connectedness cannot be ignored. However subtle this sense of sharing a common life is in the beginning, the old feeling of separation cannot be restored. One has slipped past the edges of isolation, and henceforth what happens to other living things—to some extent, at least—happens to oneself.

Aside from our own experiences, it is not so difficult envisioning relationships between humans and dogs, cats, horses, and possibly a few other species that have become familiar companions of our lives. We have come to take these sharings for granted, along with an acceptance of claims of the owner that they can communicate well with their pets. When we learn that interspecies communication has become a reality between humans and dolphins, gorillas, or chimpanzees, we are not surprised because we have been told for some time now that these particular creatures are very intelligent.

But we are less prepared when we are told that interspecies communication and even bonding can occur between humans and seemingly all other expressions of life, from mountain sheep to house flies and from barley grass to rattlesnakes. When we imagine ourselves someday arriving at a level of sensitivity and awareness where we experience a breakthrough in our oneness with life, we may see this happening with a magnificent eagle or a powerful wild stallion. A breathtaking mountain range or a Thoreau-like lake may support the scenario. But our new relationship with nature can just as easily happen on a dusty prairie trail and with a member of a species that we've even hunted as prey.

My life changed in a western Kansas milo field on a late fall day with the killing of a ringneck pheasant. I had gone hunting with my son on the opening day of pheasant season. We had each bagged a couple of birds, and my experience had been one of satisfaction in my marksmanship.

Then, not thirty feet from where I walked, a cock pheasant came up and headed low between rows of milo stalks. My 12-gauge exploded, and the bird hit the ground rolling. I reached him before he died. His wings made one last effort to carry him beyond the pain, but to no avail. For one fleeting moment he raised his head, and his eyes found mine. I will always believe that those eyes asked, "Why?" In that instant I felt his pain, and the utter waste of my action tore at me. I did not need his life in order to survive; I had killed him just for amusement. A deep sadness stayed with me for days, and I never went hunting again.

The killing of wallabies in the Australian Outback led Michael J. Roads into the experience of communication with his prey. Roads and his wife Treenie were running a herd of cattle on improved pastures, but they discovered that the organically improved grass was highly attractive to large numbers of wallabies, who came out of surrounding forests to graze on it.

Roads decided that he had to defend his pastures and started spending two nights each week shooting the encroachers. But this he found to be extremely distasteful, so he opened the pastures to hunters. When this move seemed to make little difference in the condition of the pastures, he resumed his own shooting of the wallabies.

One night he spotted a large kangaroo in his headlights and jumped out of his pickup with his rifle. But as he aimed, the animal's head swung toward him, and a shaft of light caught its eyes. "Transformed into glowing red jewels, the eyes met mine, and I gazed spellbound into the soul of a wild and wonderful Nature," Roads said. "For long moments our eyes held, locked. Slowly and calmly the animals looked away to quietly graze in the pasture."

Roads realized that the solution did not reside in violence. He talked the problem over with Treenie. Earlier, they believed that they had been successful in communicating with their cattle simply by sending them telepathic thoughts. They decided to try thought communication with the wallabies.

One morning Roads drove to the hills and stopped near a grove of trees in the center of the paddock in order to prepare himself for the attempted communication. He originally planned to send thoughts to the animals, but he found it easier to verbalize his requests, and he ended up shouting, "I don't know if you wallabies can hear me, but I am offering an agreement with you by which we each meet our own needs. I am asking you to stop eating our pasture, and in exchange for this I will see to it that nobody shoots you again. However, because I realize I must share this land with you, I will allow you to graze around the outside of the paddock. Please don't take more than twenty yards."

Roads had no idea whether anything would happen, but to keep his side of the agreement, he padlocked the entrance gate to his property and told the hunters not to shoot any more.

Within a few weeks, the pasture grew and thickened so rapidly that he was able to introduce extra cattle on the land. The wallabies crossed the pasture, but they limited their grazing to the boundaries.

For three years the agreement between Roads and the wallabies was observed, and the pasture flourished. But he explains in his book that there was a sad follow-up to the story. He sold the land and didn't tell the new owner about the agreement. . . . "Who would believe such a thing?"

When Roads visited the property three years later, the owner told him that the pasture was nearly stripped of grass and clover. The owner had started shooting wallabies again. But, "apparently, as soon as the shooting began," Roads explained, "the wallabies swarmed in, and despite six thousand shot, they literally wiped out the pasture."

Other creatures have been known to live up to agreements with humans. Some Native Americans have live-and-let-live agreements with rattlesnakes. The Navajos, for one, claim that they live in peace with the snakes and that their tribe members are never struck by the poisonous reptiles. I have seen Native Americans walk right by a rattler, and the snake doesn't even coil, but it will immediately do so when a white man approaches.

The snake may be one of the most underrated members of the animal kingdom. Although snakes have no fins, they can swim as fast as many fish, and although they have no legs, they can travel as fast as a human. Some snakes can climb a tree as ably as a monkey, but they have no hands or feet for the climb. They sleep without closing their eyes and can detect sound, although they lack complete ears with which to hear. Snakes crawl upon the ground and yet are among the cleanest of all animals.

"When you look at a snake and call it loathsome, are you not speaking of a condition within yourself?" an Indian friend of mine asked. "Look at what the snake has to work with: no hands, no feet, and yet he does very well. Do you resent this in him?"

Why do so many people shrink at the sight of a snake? According to Genesis, man was tricked by the serpent and therefore would always despise it, but this does not offer us a very plausible explanation for the behavior of most humans toward snakes. It may explain how the writer of the first book of the Bible felt toward snakes, but snakes have not always been treated so badly by cultures other than the Judeo-Christian ones.

The Native American does not respond to snakes as do most people in Western Cultures; the East Indian accepts the supernatural wisdom of the snake and the coiled serpent as the symbol of universal energy. The ancient Egyptian held snakes in high esteem and believed them to possess psychic powers that could bring good fortune to those who cared for them. The pharaohs often kept large collections of snakes, feeding and pampering them. They used the snake as a symbol of protection, and the serpent with its tail in its mouth was a symbol of infinity and the oneness of life.

The Hopi Indians of New Mexico and Arizona continue to use the snake in their annual religious ceremonies. They do not worship the snakes; rather, they believe that the creatures, being psychic, carry messages to the higher spirits. Hopi men and boys collect snakes and place them in earthenware jars. During the ceremony Indian priests dance with the snakes in their hands and even hold them with their mouths. Treated with respect and kindness, the snakes never attack their human handlers.

Snake trainer Grace Wiley and her subjects never had a problem communicating and keeping their agreements with each other. As the herpetologist at the Zoo for Happiness near Long Beach, California, she was considered one of the world's most skilled handlers of poisonous snakes with bad reputations. These included a variety of rattlers, vipers, green mambas, fer-de-lances, adders, Australian black snakes, and enormous king cobras more than twenty-five feet long. Yet she would talk softly to these dangerous characters, sending caring thoughts to them, and within hours was able to stroke and hold the snakes in her arms.

People came from all over the world to watch Grace Wiley gentle the killer reptiles. Once the snake and Wiley were in complete rapport and the snake was nestled affectionately in her arms, she would tell her audience that the creature was not really a troublemaker but a fine gentleman, that if he were to strike it would be because someone with evil intent had invaded its territory, making it feel cornered and frightened.

To begin communications with a snake, Wiley would capture the reptile and bring it to her gentling room, which was bare except for a heavy oblong table in the center. J. Allen Boone was present during one of these sessions and described it as "breathtaking." Before the snake was brought into the room, Wiley entered quietly and stood motionless against one of the walls. In one hand she held a padded stick about three feet long, known as a petting stick. In the other hand she held a stick of the same length that had a cup-like mesh used for pushing back the head of striking snakes.

Boone saw a large box wheeled into the room, and at a nod from Wiley the rear end of the box was elevated and the front end jerked off. Out slid a powerful six-foot diamondback rattler from Texas. Like a flash of lightning the big rattler coiled into an attack position, ready to take on anyone or anything that might be a threat. But there was nothing to fight; there was only the bare walls and the motionless woman facing him. The snake's head darted in every direction, trying to determine from which direction trouble might come. His tail rattled furiously, but nothing happened.

Wiley was not just passive, however. From the moment the deadly rattler slid from the box he was receiving a bombardment of powerful messages from the statue-like figure frozen against the wall. She was communicating images of respect, appreciation, admiration, affection, and gentleness. "Had your ears been attuned to the silent universal language of the heart, you would have heard in detail the flow of soundless good talk that was moving from Miss Wiley to the snake, not down at it as 'a lower form of life,' but across to it as a fellow expression of life," Boone explained.

After a time there was a marked change in the snake's attitude. The rattling of its tail stopped, and its head, instead of glaring here and there, steadied itself in the direction of the woman. The Texas killer was showing every sign of responding to the feelings and thoughts being sent in his direction.

Wiley kept up her caring and reassuring talk, now in soft but audible tones. The big snake slowly uncoiled and cautiously stretched out full-length on the table, finally resting its head within inches of the trainer's body. She then moved for the first time, slowly stroking the rattler's back with the padded stick. When she found no resistance in the snake, she stroked him then with her bare hands. "And as you watched this almost unbelievable performance," Boone stated, "you would have seen the snake arch its long back in catlike undulations, in order better to feel the affection-filled ministrations."

This kind of communication and bonding apparently happened between John Solomon Rorey and wild horses others believed too mean and unpredictable to handle. During the middle of the nineteenth century the break-

ing of horses—or, for that matter, the training of any animals—was based on fear. But Rorey, whom the press
called the world's greatest wild horse trainer, got along
with the worst of the lot, using love, kindness, and an
amazing ability to understand the thoughts and feelings
of his students. Ralph Waldo Emerson once said of him:
"John Rorey has turned a new leaf for civilization."

No one ever knew Rorey's secret, for he always
insisted on being alone when he tamed a wild horse. His
talent emerged when he was twelve years old. His father,
Adam Rorey, had brought home to their farm near
Columbus, Ohio, an incorrigible colt. It was well-bred
but cheap, because the former owner had given up on
him after a dozen professional horse-breakers failed to
tame the animal. Deciding to show the colt who was
boss, Adam struck him with a whip. The horse reacted
by snapping his halter rope and slamming the man
against a fence with such violence that he broke his leg.

Convinced the horse was insane, Adam ordered one
of his hands to shoot him. The man, along with some
neighbors, headed for the barn, but before they arrived
young Rorey emerged from the barn astride the animal
that no one had been able to get close to.

Rorey's fame spread quickly after this incident. Horses
from all over the country were brought to him to break. If
he kept them a few days, he also would teach them to bow,
kneel, and canter. At the age of nineteen, Rorey was challenged in Texas to conquer five of the meanest horses the
Texans could round up. Four of the horses had each killed
a man, and the fifth had crippled two men.

Thousands gathered to watch what they believed to
be the death of the legendary Rorey. He ignored the bet-

ting odds against him and entered the box stall holding the first killer while the audience gasped. As the minutes passed the odds went higher and higher in favor of the horses. But forty minutes later Rorey rode the horse out of the stall and to the center of the corral. While the crowd roared in astonishment, he dismounted, had the killer kneel and then lie on its side. The other horses were to follow with similar performances.

Internationally famous, Rorey traveled the country demonstrating that the most dangerous horse could be tamed and lecturing on the importance of kindness to animals. He traveled throughout Europe and tamed the meanest horses in France, Germany, Sweden, England, Spain, and Egypt.

In England in 1868 Rorey was challenged to tame Lord Dorchester's former racing stallion, Cruiser, who for four years had been considered completely insane. At times the horse became so violent that it bit itself and tore a wooden rail stall to pieces. It was kept in a specially constructed brick-and-steel stall.

When the group of titled persons, sportsmen, and news reporters arrived with Rorey at Cruiser's stall, the horse was attacking the door in such a frenzy that the entire structure shook. Lord Dorchester suddenly realized that he might well be responsible for Rorey's death, so he offered to withdraw the challenge and to pay Rorey for his trouble and trip.

Rorey told Dorchester that he needn't be concerned, that all he would need was a halter and a body belt. When the horse was momentarily dazed from striking his head against the stall, Rorey slipped inside and put the halter on the horse and slipped out again. The crazed animal then attacked the halter, which was attached to a ring in the wall, until he dropped from exhaustion. Rorey slipped in again and snapped on the body belt with two straps. It was so arranged that Rorey could buckle the horse's front legs by pulling on the straps.

Rorey sat beside the horse for three hours, petting it, stroking its neck, and talking softly to it. Whenever Cruiser struggled, Rorey gently pulled on the straps. The following day Rorey rode Cruiser through the streets of London.

John Solomon Rorey died at the age of thirty-eight, but his legend and, more important, his message lives on in the hearts and minds of those who believe that real respect and love for life, whatever form it takes, can open the door to understanding and communication between species.

An interspecies communication link was forged by John Gambill with Canadian geese simply by virtue of his caring. He nursed a wounded gander back to health at his Gambill Wild Goose Reservation near Paris, Texas. The following autumn the gander returned with twelve geese that became quite tame.

The next year the number of geese was in excess of a hundred, and by the time that Gambill died in 1962 probably more than three hundred geese wintered in safety on the reservation. As life slipped away from Gambill in a Paris hospital, hundreds of geese from the reservation flew into the town of Paris and circled around and around the hospital, honking their requiem.

The act of caring also established a bond between a medical doctor and a female bighorn sheep, who during the summer of 1962 came down from the high country to the town of Mt. Baldy, California. The ewe was very sick, but the doctor found the animal and nursed her back to health. Once well, she returned to the mountains, but ten months later she brought her ailing newborn lamb to the doctor's home: unable to heal the lamb herself, she had come back to the man who could help.

Eldon Bisbee is convinced that the spirit of a deceased dog saved the life of his French poodle by communicating with a taxicab driver. One night the cab driver came to the door of Bisbee's New York City home carrying Bisbee's injured poodle. The driver told Bisbee that he had been driving through a snowstorm when he was stopped by a German shepherd, who refused to get out of the way. The cab driver shouted at the animal, but it came to his car window and whined and then ran to a snow bank, so the cab driver got out of his car and discovered the injured poodle with the shepherd standing over her, wagging his tail. The driver picked up the poodle and put her in his car, and the shepherd stayed in front of the car, leading the way down the street, finally running up onto the sidewalk leading to Bisbee's house. When the driver stopped the car and headed toward the house, the shepherd just seemed to disappear, he told Bisbee.

A close bond between two other dogs, along with one dog's confidence in a caring physician, led to the second dog's healing. Dr. W. F. Sturgill, physician for the Norfolk and Western Railroad, once treated a friend's dog for an injury suffered on barbed wire. About a year later he heard a scratching on his door and opened it to discover his friend's dog, but with him was another dog with injured and bleeding paws. The doctor took care of the injuries, and the dogs trotted off together!

Rags was the only inhabitant of Sing Sing Prison who was there by choice. The small mongrel, part

Scottie and part wire-haired terrier, turned herself in at the gray somber walls during a cold autumn day in 1929 and spent the next twelve years communicating with the prisoners. Rags spent her days cheering up the dismal atmosphere of the prison. She worked out a set of tricks, stunts, mimicry, and acrobatics to entertain the men. A large part of each day was spent making the rounds of the shops, the cell blocks, and the hospital.

Rags befriended all the inmates but was careful never to show partiality to anyone. She completely ignored the guards and any visitors. Each day she ate at a different table in the mess hall, rotating systematically in order not to miss a table. She left the prison compound at the end of the day to sleep in the warden's home but returned in the evening if there was going to be entertainment or a performance, never failing to know when this would be. Warden Frank Lawes ordered the guards to let her in and out of the locked doors whenever she wished.

Rags was particularly sensitive to a despondent, brooding prisoner. She would rub her head against him, perform all kinds of acts to cheer him up, and then lead him to a group so he would not be alone.

One night Rags did not leave the cell blocks. She followed one of the prisoners to his cell and remained in front of it until morning. The prisoner had been refused a pardon and, discouraged, had decided that no one cared what happened to him. He was determined to end it all that night by hanging himself with his bed sheet.

Rags never gave the man that chance. Every time he tried to slip out of his bunk, the dog growled, and the prisoner knew that if he went any farther Rags would bark and bring the guard on the run. He finally decided that at least Rags cared what happened to him and that he would give himself another chance.

In the annals of interspecies communication and animal intelligence, the case of Missie, a Boston terrier, is mind-boggling, for we are forced to re-evaluate our schematics of levels and degrees of awareness possessed by certain species. Missie doesn't fit into these accepted concepts.

To identify Missie as the pet of Mildred Probert somehow seems inappropriate. It seems more accurate to say that the two were close companions and friends. The dog came into Probert's life shortly after it was born. Because the puppy was so tiny it was not kept with the litter. Probert, who had retired from floral design work and was keeping pets who needed special care, had the tiny puppy bestowed on her. She said that Missie never learned to associate with or care for other animals. The terrier remained small and, unlike the rest of her breed, had deep cobalt eyes.

Missie was four years old before Probert became aware of her special qualities. One day Probert and her mother were walking with the dog when they came upon an acquaintance with her small child in tow. They asked the child his age. The child didn't answer, and the mother explained that he was timid, but that he was three. Probert leaned over the child and said, "Three. Say, 'three.'" The child remained silent but Missie barked three times. Everyone laughed and Probert said, "Okay, Smarty, how old are you?" The dog barked four times. More than a little surprised, Probert asked, "How old will you be next week?" Five distinct barks followed—an accurate report.

"That was the beginning," Probert told me. "It really wasn't a matter of training her, for she knew things that I didn't. It was just a matter of trying to find out what she knew." What Missie knew seemed endless. Through testing, Probert learned that Missie could add. The owner didn't know how the terrier learned to cope with numbers; she had developed her system entirely on her own. If a series of street numbers were involved, she would bark so many times for the first number, pause, bark out the second number, and so on.

Missie's uncanniness with numbers included not only addition and subtraction but the number of letters in a word or name. Her extraordinary powers were discovered when a stranger to both Missie and her owner asked the dog to tell him his address. She barked out the numbers without hesitation. Probert found that she could ask Missie to tell her how many letters were in the first name of a person she herself didn't know. Missie would bark out the correct number and would follow this with the number of letters in the last name. She was constantly being tested, and she could give correct answers whether Probert was in the room or not.

At parties, Missie could be relied on to tell people how many coins were in their purses or how many beans were in a sack. Often those present did not know the number beforehand. Missie would also correctly bark out the number of spots on a playing card without seeing the face of the card.

Missie figured out a way of answering yes and no. She would bark two times for "no" and shake her head sideways, and bark three times for "yes" and shake her head up and down.

A skeptical physician friend was having a difficult

time accepting Missie's unusual abilities. "Well, Doctor, there is one number that neither Missie nor I know and that is your private home number," Probert said to him. When Missie barked out the correct number, the physician leaned back in his chair perplexed. On another occasion Probert asked a doubting news reporter, "What is your social security number?" When he couldn't remember, Missie correctly barked out the number.

The small dog's ability to predict the future was discovered one day in the fall of 1964 as Missie and her owner were visiting in a store where people were in the habit of asking the dog questions. When Missie predicted the outcome of the presidential race between Lyndon Johnson and Barry Goldwater and turned out to be an accurate forecaster, the *Rocky Mountain News* carried the story, and that was the beginning of many predictions related to local and world news.

The dog correctly predicted the number of delays in the launching of Gemini 12, space probes, and moon landings. On New Year's Eve of 1965 an interviewer on Denver's KTLN radio station asked Missie when the New York transit strike would end, and she barked out "January 13," which proved to be correct. On another radio station, the dog with the penetrating blue eyes predicted nine months in advance the outcome of the World Series, the day the series would end, and the correct score.

Missie's knowledge of future events seemed as vast as the imagination of those asking the questions. She foretold in her own ineffable fashion the failure of the atom-smashing plant to be located in Denver, the date for the initiation of the Paris Peace Talks and their outcome, and the date of the return of the Colorado

National Reserve from the Vietnam War. She became a regular on a number of radio talk shows. The London Daily Call called her "the best psychic in America."

To one salesman, at least, Missie was a virtual library. He came knocking on Probert's door, wanting to sell her a set of encyclopedias. "I have a walking one right here," she told him. "What do you want to know?" Once he adjusted himself to the situation and decided to humor his potential buyer, the salesman settled on the subject of the Civil War and asked a number of questions. Without hesitation, the answers came back from the pint-size genius in front of him. "I guess you're right, lady," he said, packing up his samples and shaking his head.

Mildred Probert told us about her life with Missie as we sat in the living room of her old Victorian home in Denver. By that time, however, the dog had been dead several years, and another Boston terrier, Sissy, kept inviting me to play with her. Probert explained that Sissy was not psychic.

While talking about the years since Missie's death, Probert told us that Missie had predicted the hour of her own death. Missie always knew the time, would bark out the hour and even the minutes. A friend had made her a toy clock with hands that the small dog could move. To set the clock she always moved the hands in a clockwise fashion. On the day of her death in May, 1966, a few days before her eleventh birthday, Missie kept calling Probert's attention to the time, but she would bark eight o'clock. Since it was not that time, Probert would ask her what time it was on the clock. Missie would then bark the correct time but would immediately go back to barking eight o'clock. At exactly eight o'clock in the evening Missie died, choking on a piece of food. All efforts to save her were to no avail. Later her owner discovered the dog's toy clock in a corner of the room. The hands had been turned to eight o'clock.

So many times since—when my attention is captured by a dog playing patiently with a small child in a park, or when I have looked up to see my own dog studying my face, or perhaps when I have slipped into a philosophical mood in my den late at night—I have found myself thinking about Missie. She remains, of course, an enigma, for how can we find plausible reasons for her behavior and achievements? We can only speculate.

It would seem that we are faced with one of two choices. Either we have completely underestimated the intelligence of dogs, along with their psychic skills, or Missie was, in essence, was not a dog, but a dog's body was simply serving as an earth vehicle for a higher intelligence.

If the former, it is thought-provoking to ponder the implications of future discoveries in animal behavior, most likely as they evolve from accelerated interspecies communication rather than laboratory research. If the latter, why would an advanced intelligence choose a canine body through which to incarnate? To deliver a message to humans concerning the value of other life forms on this planet? To humble us and force us to rethink our treatment of other creatures? Maybe one day we'll know.

Yet there is a bottom line to both arguments. Whichever we choose, we are closer to the position that mind is something other than and not limited to the organic brain. Further, the capabilities of the mind are not limited by the brain, nervous system, and body structure. Although the expressions of the mind may be restricted by lack of complex verbal expression, the omission of a thumb opposite the fingers, and other features, behind the animal system may be an intelligence far superior to those levels we have assigned it.

Thank God for such visionary persons as Michael Roads, Grace Wiley. John Solomon Rorey, John Gambill, and Mildred Probert, who help us to be open to the possibilities.

12

Small Communicators

When we consider interspecies communication we usually think in terms of human-creature exchanges or interactions in which some kind of relationship has been established. But it is not uncommon for us to experience—or to know of those who experience—an interaction with members of the plant kingdom. Occasionally we expand our definition of communication to include those individuals who understand other life expressions or forces of nature, such as the wind, the rain, or the waves crashing on a beach.

Seldom, however, do we include insects as fellow communicators, as inhabitants of this planet with whom we would want to listen or to talk. With the exception of bees, earthworms, ladybugs, praying mantises, and a few other acceptable species, our usual response to insects is to ignore or to annihilate them. Most people, if they could, would deny insects planetary citizenship.

Yet, in the final analysis, life on earth would be

impossible without insects; they are essential links in the ecological chain. While people grudgingly accept this fact, they are not anxious to share in other ways. Those who have learned in some manner to interact with these small residents, however, have been amazed by their intelligence.

One of the most fascinating stories of the rapport between man and an insect was J. Allen Boone's relationship with a common housefly he called Freddie. Boone made friends with the fly, and it would join him each morning at seven o'clock by landing on his shaving mirror. Boone would invite him to climb aboard his finger and he would gently stroke the fly's wings. Freddie paraded up and down his finger, and they would play a game in which Boone tossed the fly in the air and caught him again on the tip of his finger.

The early-morning rendezvous between fly and human continued for some time, and the small housefly would also come when Boone called his name. Remembering what he had learned from the wise German shepherd Strongheart, Boone reminded himself first that inherently, Freddie the fly and himself as living beings were inseparable parts of an interrelated, interfunctioning, and all-including Totality, and second that neither the fly nor he were originating causes for anything but were instead individual living expressions of a universal divine Cause or Mind that was ever speaking and living itself through each of them and through everything else. He was to discover, as he had with other creatures, that much was to be learned by "silently talking across to him. Not as to 'a fly' with all the limiting and condemning things that we humans usually fasten on flies, but as to an intelligent fellow being."

In order to truly appreciate Boone's experience with Freddie, we seem to be required to adopt a shift in consciousness. The experience can be viewed as a bizarre and isolated experience with an insect, or it can be understood as communication between two expressions of God. Meister Eckhart would most likely have accepted the latter, for he once stated:

"When I preached in Paris I said then—and I regard it well said—that not a man in Paris can conceive with all his learning that God is in the very meanest of creatures—even in a fly."

Communication between beekeepers and their bees has a long history in Europe. When a beekeeper died, it was the custom to let the bees know, in a ceremony called "telling the bees." Sometimes the beehive was draped in black crepe. Following this ancient custom, after Sam Rogers, a cobbler and postman of the Shropshire village of Myddle, England, died, his children walked around his fourteen hives and told his bees. Newspapers reported that shortly after relatives of Rogers gathered at his grave, thousands of bees from Rogers' hives more than a mile away came and settled on and about the coffin. The bees entirely ignored the flowering trees nearby. They stayed for about half an hour and then returned to the hives.

If the awareness of any creature, regardless of size or form, is simply an expression of the universal consciousness, then perhaps it should not surprise us that a research chemist would attribute his success in the laboratory to his ability to gain rapport with the bacteria and other forms of micro-organisms with which he worked.

This was the case with J. William Jean, who acquired

a considerable reputation for the many unusual and useful things he produced in his Pasadena, California, laboratory. His success arose from his firm conviction that all beings, regardless of how humans are accustomed to define and classify them, are God's purpose in action. The second was his mental attitude toward his tiny business partners: an attitude of friendliness, admiration, respect, encouragement, and limitless expectancy. As well, he was able to understand and co-operate with them, and as a result the bacteria and his other micro-organic associates reacted favorably to this kind of treatment. Apparently, Jean's spirit of high adventure in his work and his friendly identification with everything that lives allowed him to make practical and successful use of invisible bridges for helpful two-way thought traffic between himself and his tiny workers. These were both mental bridges, between intelligences, and intuitive bridges, built upon that speech that does not have to be uttered.

Newspapers have for several years reported on a young Brazilian youth, Francisco Duarte, who is allegedly able to give instructions to all kinds of animals and insects. Small for his age and considered mentally retarded, Duarte handles spiders, wasps, bees, snakes, frogs, rats, and alligators without being bitten or even attacked. Further, according to Alvaro Fernandes, a Brazilian parapsychology investigator, all the animals obey the instructions given to them by the youth.

According to the reports of Francisco and those provided by investigator Martha Barros, bees, for example, will land where Duarte tells them to, and if he tells all the bees except six, to return to the hive, that is what happens. Poisonous snakes will coil, uncoil, or move to where he tells them, and fish will come to his hand in the water when he tells them to do so. Duarte told reporter Michael Joy, "I talk to the animals, and they talk to me. I can understand everything they say. My talent is a gift from God."

The secret of life is that there is continuous communication not only between living things and their environment but among all things living in the environment. An intricate web of interaction connects all life into one vast, self-maintaining system. "There is life on earth," biologist Lyall Watson tells us in *Supernature*, "one life, which embraces every animal and plant on the planet. Time has divided it up into several million parts, but each is an integral part of the whole. A rose is a rose, but it is also a robin and a rabbit. We are all part of one flesh, drawn from the same crucible."

The evidence on hand indicates that there is an awareness beyond the so-called normal senses. This awareness puts the subject not only in contact with his or her immediate environment but also with things and events at some distance. If this is the case, then life, regardless of the form it takes, is part of a universal and unifying consciousness. Each thing is related to everything else, and each life form can, to some lesser or greater degree, affect and be influenced by everything in the universe.

13

The Song of Life

Communication with creatures other than ourselves may be not only important but even critical to our own survival. If interspecies communication goes mainstream—that is, becomes generally accepted by the public at large as the natural outcome of a greater understanding—then we will have good reason to believe in the future of this planet. If, on the other hand, interspecies communication remains in most people's minds isolated phenomena occurring for unknown reasons to a few unusual individuals, then we have every reason to be concerned about the earth and its inhabitants.

To me our lack of awareness that all species save us human beings communicate naturally with each other reveals our failure to grasp the truth that all life is connected—that everything is related to everything in existence. What affects one life form affects others. It seems to me that those who cannot comprehend this are not only out of touch with nature but also out of touch with themselves and with God. This is serious business.

Interspecies communication becomes a matter of the parts recognizing their kinship with the other parts and the whole. But, in the final analysis, perhaps it is less a matter of demonstrating that animals and plants are intelligent and capable of communication than it is to come to the realization that all life is a creation of and within God, the All Conscious. More accurately, interspecies communication goes far beyond someone talking to plants and another listening to dolphins: it has to do with humanity communicating with God. It is a matter of our ability, or inability, to go to the Source of all information. A nature spirit is one of God's expressions; a human is another, as is a tree, the wind, a wolf, an eagle. If we cannot comprehend this, we have isolated ourselves from all other life and from God. We have also become exceedingly dangerous to ourselves and all other expressions of life.

What occurs when we communicate with an orca whale or find ourselves in rapport with the spirit of a tree is a person talking to and listening to God. Gary Kowalski knows this: ". . . because all life shares in One Spirit, we can recognize this indwelling beauty in other creatures," he suggests. "Animals, like us, are microcosms. They too care and have feelings; they too dream and create; they too are adventuresome and curious about their world. They too reflect the glory of the whole."

It is not so difficult to believe that all living entities, like humans, possess not only an outer physical form but an inner spiritual component. Frank Waters, one of the foremost writers on the Native American, stated in an

interview several years ago that humans must graduate
to this belief, "to attune ourselves to both the inner and
outer realities of life if we are to close the widening rupture between our minds and hearts." By "rupture"
Waters meant that humans, in destroying nature, were
also destroying themselves. He pointed out that our
unconscious is equated to and rooted in nature, and that
we have, by our destructive and materialistic rationalism,
alienated our conscious selves from the earliest substra-
tum of our essential being.

What was so hauntingly beautiful about *Jonathan
Livingston Seagull* was not that the book was a modern
mythology presenting hidden truths in an allegorical fashion—certainly, it was this—but while one understood that
the story pertained to man's sojourn upon this and other
worlds, the readers were almost equally sure that the story
was also about seagulls. We would tell ourselves that it was
not, committed as we are to the Judeo-Christian belief that
immortality is reserved for our own species; but something
within our unconscious domains, or at the intuitive level of
our hearts, tells us we share our destiny with the great white
bird. The delight and optimism we experienced in reading
the words, which Richard Bach himself claimed came to
him from another dimension, defied any logical convictions
to the contrary, and we found ourselves basking at least for
the moment in a certain knowledge that all of life is one.

The Biblical Job tells us, "But ask now the beasts,
and they shall teach thee, and the fowls of the air, and
they shall tell thee. . . ." But we have a tendency to
equate communication with words, even assigning
descriptive phrases to music and art, forgetting that these
means of expression are language in themselves. If we

are to comment accurately on music, we must do so with music, and to a painting we must respond with a painting. Words have made us forget our beginnings. We have used them to chronicle our experiences through the ages. They have been the building blocks of civilizations. But they have taken us away from ourselves, and we have imagined that to label something is to understand it. Words have been our passport out of Eden, but they have served to alienate us from the other inhabitants of this planet.

Perhaps we have underestimated the intelligence of animals and nature spirits because we have imagined that our concepts of achievement are the only ones, that the development of technology and the establishment of a complex civilization are the only indicators of growth. We have envisioned that the only intelligence is our kind: God has an infinite amount of it, and animals have a small amount, but it is a matter of degree, not of kind. Since we assumed that the so-called lower creatures had nothing to teach us, we have not listened. Because of our own myopia and inadequacies, we have lived in the world, but a great deal of it has passed us by.

My German shepherd Baron had his own way of gaining my attention and seeing to it that I didn't let the world about me slip by unnoticed. One early evening on a hike through a meadow, Baron suddenly stopped and sat down in front of me. I tried to move past him, but he placed himself in front of me again, and I realized he was trying to tell me something. He kept looking at me until I, too, sat down in the grass, and then he turned away from me and gazed at the setting sun. His eyes fixed to the West, he sat immobile until a while after the sun had set. When he came out of his reverie, he nudged

me, and we took off again across the meadow, he playfully, myself in thought, in awe.

Earlier, while in my early teens, I had a similar experience with another companion, a great horned owl. I
called the bird Yahoote. I had captured him while trap-
ping for furs, but after a few days of anger, his hostility
passed miraculously, and we became quite close. During
his non-preying daylight hours he would sit on my shoulder or stay close by.

Early one evening, with Yahoote perched on my
shoulder, I was walking along a cattle trail facing East.
Although the owl always faced the same direction as I did,
on this occasion he turned around and faced West. As he
did so, he made a muffled sound in his throat. Finding
that I was not paying attention, Yahoote shuffled his claws
and saw to it that I felt their sharpness. Again he made
the strange throaty sound. Thinking that he had spotted
something behind me, I turned, and the owl did also.
There in the western sky was one of the most uniquely
beautiful sunsets I had ever seen. I sat down on the prairie
grass to watch. Yahoote was satisfied. We both waited
quietly until the last rose and lavender faded from the sky.

A special communication link sometimes occurs
between humans and their animal companions. The
experience is not easy to capture with words but might
be described as a sharing of essence. Once known, its
loss is difficult to accept. This happened to Martin
Buber, according to his biographer, M. Friedman. When
he was a boy, Buber and a dapple-grey mare had a special affinity for each other. But one day while he was
stroking the horse, he became aware of his own hand,
and with a start he realized that the link between him

and the horse was broken. Buber's attention had wandered from the horse itself to his own thoughts about the horse. In that instant he was no longer relating to the horse as a friend but was thinking of the horse as an object, a thing. The mare also sensed the change. When Buber returned to the stall the next day, the horse no longer raised its head in greeting. He continued to pet the horse, but the relationship had changed.

We have a long history of treating animals as things or objects. They have become commodities to us. They serve our turn or fulfill our needs as sources of food, clothing, work, laboratory subjects, and so on. Even as pets, they are there to amuse us, and animals in zoos serve to satisfy our curiosity. Kowalski points out that we "de-sacralize" animals, that we "rob them of their holy qualities—and in the process de-humanize ourselves. For animals cannot be relegated to the status of objects. When we treat them as if they were mere biological machines—collections of conditioned reflexes—we injure both their nature and our own."

As we ponder the experiences of those who have shared deeply with species other than our own, all life appears to be one, the expression of some all-pervading intelligence. Nothing short of this would allow for the love of the collie Bobbie for her human family. They were driving from Ohio to their new home in Oregon when Bobbie wandered away and became lost during a rest stop in Indiana. Three months later, a thin and battered Bobbie showed up at the doorstep of the family's new Oregon home, a place she had never been. Bobbie's odyssey is like others we've all read in newspapers, but that does not distract from their impressiveness. The evidence seems to point to a Universal Mind in which all life has its being. Would this explain Missie's ability to foresee the future? or how Rags understood that unless he kept vigil a despondent prisoner would take his own life? or how dogs could return from the dead to warn their former masters of danger?

The great German shepherd Strongheart made such an impression on J. Allen Boone, movie director and producer, that the sharing changed his life. In trying to understand their ability to communicate with one another, Allen stated: "Strongheart and I were mental beings before we could possibly be objectified as material expressions of life. Therefore it was as mental beings that the dog and I had rightly to relate ourselves in order to have the rest of us rightly related, too. Whenever I worked it from this angle, Strongheart and I always moved in perfect accord."

If all creatures are equally expressions of God, then where does this position put us as regards animal rights? Do animals have rights? Oren Long, who has thought about and written on the subject, suggests that animals have rights but only those rights we choose to give them. As to whether animals have inherent rights, he argues that they do not, and that neither do we. "Americans have inherent rights simply because we say so. Then we wrote them into our most basic political documents. Then we passed laws and established institutions to help guarantee such rights. In other words, as humans we have only those 'rights' which we have the power to guarantee for ourselves."

Animals, on the other hand, do not have the power to guarantee rights for themselves. And so the question becomes: What rights should we grant to animals? Long explains that this is an important question, because "there can be no better measure of a man's character than the rights, or treatment, he gives his animals."

If we have the power to extend or withhold rights to our own kind and other creatures, how do we determine to whom or to what? Won't our choices —as well as our power to exercise these choices—eventually affect our own rights?

Many sincere and dedicated persons argue that our highest priority should be to help humankind. In other words, children before pets, people before animals, human needs before conservation. But as Dr. Michael Fox points out in his book *One Earth, One Mind*, such priorities reflect a limited world view that lacks a global ethical framework embracing all forms of life and that fails to see the vital interdependence of all life.

If we concern ourselves only with the human species or with a select few endangered species in which we choose some over others, we are making value judgments. And Dr. Fox points out that "A transpersonal ethic of reverence for all life makes no such evaluations." If we consider humans more important than the other inhabitants of the earth, then logically we would have to judge which humans are of greater or lesser value than others. "The result is an artificial, hierarchical outlook," Dr. Fox states. "Reverence for all transcends this ethical bind, which is a flaw in many religions and philosophies today. . . . Some see only human suffering as needing to be rectified, but I believe all destruction and suffering are interrelated, since human problems affect all life forms."

These sentiments echo those of psychiatrist Rollo May when he states: "Loss of the relation to nature goes hand in hand with the loss of the sense of one's own self. 'Little we see in nature that is ours,' as a description of many modern people, is a mark of the weakened and impoverished person."

Down through the ages, of course, only some humans were recognized as having rights. Sovereignty has often been limited to such royal overlords as heads of state and dictators, who alone determined the extent and rights held by others. In most nations today control still remains in the hands of a few. Until recent years, only adult males could vote, and not long ago the males had to be property owners and of a certain race. For centuries, women, slaves, and to some extent children were chattel or property to be disposed of according to the whims of the owner. This is largely the position that animals are in today. Will animal rights ever become a major issue? The answer will likely depend on what we learn about creatures other than ourselves, what their position—along with ours—is in the universe.

But if our considerations of animals were directed to the welfare of humankind alone, the priority would be reasonably high, not because of a balance in nature or from the roles animals play in our food production but because our treatment of animals is important to our own internal state. If we are to expand our horizons, to grow, to understand what the new physics means by the relatedness of each and every living thing, then our love and appreciation of all life is essential. In a world where feelings and thoughts are things, our respect and reverence for all livings things will be reflected in our own selves.

And what if an animal learns to communicate in human words or signs and can converse about its wants, hopes, fears, thoughts, and sense of self-identity? Can it still be considered "animal" and subjected to captivity and research? The question is no longer academic and speculative; it has become a moral and practical concern for those involved in programs to teach language to animals.

Chimpanzees in one study, for example, used "if-then" concepts, persuaded humans to supply them with desired new words, manipulated people verbally to carry out their wishes, anticipated future events, joked, played tricks, expressed feelings, invented swear words, and even lied. One chimp used 251 different signs for words during a single hour of "talk."

Such experiments make it obvious that at least chimpanzees, gorillas, other apes, dolphins, whales, and possibly other species are more intelligent, more "human" in the working of their brains than we have heretofore understood. In teaching them a means of communicating with us directly by words and in learning to listen to them as they endeavor to communicate with us, how does our relationship with them change? What becomes our responsibility to them?

Referring to the successful studies in interspecies communication, columnist Joan Beck stated: "It's increasingly evident that these animals are the most intelligent non-human life forms we will ever find in our solar system. Certainly we owe it to ourselves—as well as to them—to learn all we can about communicating with them and to keep this planet a place where they can survive in some new relationship with humans. Mankind needs all the friends it can get."

Despite their fur, hooves, beaks, fins, and claws, we are going to have to accept our fellow inhabitants of this planet as something far more useful than just props in our environment. What if we were to learn that other creatures could provide us information we didn't already possess and knowledge that would be useful in our lives? What if, while we are teaching them our language, they found a way to teach us theirs, and as a result of this communication breakthrough we realized that these other creatures were equal or superior to ourselves?

It is not so difficult to imagine spaceships landing on earth and their crews, finding us very primitive in comparison to themselves, saying to one another, "Well, it's not as though they feel or have any real intelligence." To them, we would be considered second-class citizens, and they might easily decide that it was foolish to extend us any meaningful rights. Perhaps this scenario is far-fetched, and yet that is exactly how we have treated other living entities on this planet.

Will the growing body of information provided by interspecies communication studies prod our consciences as to the withholding of animal rights? Will we hold ourselves responsible for their deaths? Will we no longer be willing to slaughter them for food? Will the human race be better or worse off because of these insights? And what if we were to learn that all life forms are progressing toward a spiritual awakening, that animals pass in and out of physical form, as we do, over the course of a long history in the pursuit of some divine perfection?

It is not consciousness that grows old, deteriorates, and dies but the physical body, which serves as a vehicle for the consciousness. From a physical standpoint it seems that life is unfolding, but in reality life is ideating by overcoming the limitations of the form it occupies. Evolution makes possible the production of vehicles suitable to the needs of the beings that occupy them.

All things reveal life because life is in them, and all things move toward the fulfillment of their own eternity because eternity is in them, Manly Palmer Hall has told us, and he asks, "Can God destroy that which he has created? Is life expendable or is it eternal? To those who assume that life, consciousness, and reality are all synonymous terms, there can be no death without compromising the existence of God." And Hall argues that if there is no death, it applies not only to man but to any creature.

Whatever happens to them on this planet, the spirits of the wolf, the eagle, the tree, will survive, and somewhere they will push on in their pursuit of divine perfection. And as for our lives on earth, perhaps we will survive the extinction of many of the world's animals and plants; but when they are gone, part of us is also gone. Their ways of living, of coping, of caring, of playing, of delighting in life are also lost within ourselves. Their vitality and contributions to the matrix of the natural environment will have ceased for them and for us, and how many pieces of ourselves can we afford to lose? The substitutes we use to replace them may fill the gaps in the ecological chain, but will these synthetics repair the damage to the creative richness of the earth and the expressions missing from our souls?

As I bring this book to a close, our black cat Sara jumps up on my lap, her large yellow eyes studying my face. Is she trying to pass along thoughts she feels should be in the book or to remind me that her food pan is empty? Obviously, there is a need here for better interspecies communication! But Sara is persistent and will get her message across some way.

Outside, Marley and Mindy are howling and running, probably in pursuit of a squirrel skilled in calculating their speed versus its own and the distance to the maple trees. The game will be played out by their raising a fracas at the base of the tree and the squirrel chattering back from twenty feet up. They all understand one another. After ten minutes or so the dogs will get bored and will decide to explore the meadow or the old barn, and the squirrel will resume its pursuit of walnuts.

Now and then a cardinal flies past my window, looking for Winter fare, and the sparrows argue over evening nesting places in the cedars. In the distance I can barely hear the coyotes howling because a train has passed a mile away. They apparently don't care for the sound, or maybe it hurts their ears. No doubt Marley and Mindy will shortly find it important to answer them. Most likely, the reply is expected.

I glance down at Sara, and she looks up at me. Can either of us doubt that we need one another?

Bibliography

Bach, R. *Jonathan Livingston Seagull*. New York: Macmillan, 1970.

Blair, L. *Rhythms of Vision*. New York: Schocken, 1975.

Boone, J. A. *Kinship with All Life*. New York: Harper & Row, 1975.

Boyd, D. *Rolling Thunder*. New York: Dell, 1974.

Burbank, L. *The Training of the Human Plant*. New York: Century, 1922.

Butler, A. *Lives of the Saints*. London: Rider & Company, 1926.

Cerminara, G. *Many Lives, Many Loves*. New York: William Stone Associates, 1963.

Chesterson, G. K. *St. Francis of Assisi*. Garden City, New York: Doubleday, 1928.

Darwin, C. *Descent of Man*. New York: A. L. Burt, 1874.

———. *The Variations of Animals and Plants Under Domestication*. New York: New American Library, 1970.

Droscher, V. *The Friendly Beast.* New York: E. P. Dutton, 1971.

Ebon, F. *The Evidence of Life after Death.* New York: New American Library, 1970.

Edwards, F. *Strange World.* New York: Lyle Stuart, Inc., 1964.

Fichtelius, E. and Sjolander, S. *Smarter Than Man?* New York: Ballantine, 1974.

Fossey, D. *Gorillas in the Mist.* Boston: Houghton Mifflin, 1983.

Fulop-Miller, R. *The Saints that Moved the World.* New York: Collier, 1945.

Gaddis, V. and M. *The Strange World of Animals and Pets.* New York: Cowles, 1970.

Kowalski, G. *The Souls of Animals.* Walpole, New Hampshire: Stillpoint Publishing, 1984.

Watson, L. *Supernature.* Garden City, New York: Doubleday, 1973.

————. *The Romeo Error.* Garden City, New York: Doubleday, 1974.

White, J. *Frontiers of Consciousness.* New York: Avon, 1974.

Wright, M. *Behaving as if the God in All Life Mattered.* Jeffersonton, Virginia: Perelandra, 1987.

Yogananda, P. *The Autobiography of a Yogi.* New York: Rider, 1950.

Young, M. *Agartha: A Journey to the Stars.* Walpole, New Hampshire: Stillpoint Publishing, 1984.

Zukav, G. *The Seat of the Soul.* New York: Simon & Schuster, 1989.

If you were inspired by Life Song, *you may also wish to read:*

The Souls of Animals
by Gary Kowalski, $8.95 (Ten full-page B&W photographs by Art Wolfe)

"Gary Kowalski helps us unlock the mysteries of animal spirituality. For as we have learned from the companion animals that share our lives and our homes, when we look into their eyes we see the reflection of our own humanity."

— KIM STALLWOOD, EXECUTIVE DIRECTOR
PEOPLE FOR THE ETHICAL TREATMENT OF ANIMALS

"This is an important book because it is so revealing of the animal soul that touches ours when we are open and receptive. In the process, our own souls are enriched."

— DR. MICHAEL W. FOX, VICE PRESIDENT
THE HUMANE SOCIETY OF THE UNITED STATES

Beyond Words: Unlocking the Secrets to Communicating
by Patricia St.John, $13.95

Beyond Words is the riveting story of Patricia St.John's journey into the nonverbal world of dolphins and children with autism. It will interest and inspire anyone who is intrigued by the connection between trust, expanded sensory perception and communication, and will help you to discover your own untapped ability to interpret the unspoken messages of people and animals.

"St.John's book is about breaking down boundaries between species, people and senses. She succeeds!"

—THE SANTA FE SUN

Ask for these books at your favorite local bookstore or order them directly from Stillpoint by calling or writing:
Stillpoint Publishing
PO Box 640, Walpole, NH 03608
1-800-847-4014 (toll-free)

To Our Readers

As publishers we seek to live in ways that lighten our human load on the Earth's natural systems and our global environment.

This book is printed on chlorine-free recycled paper (minimum 10% post consumer waste) to save trees and to encourage pulp and paper companies to convert to production processes that do not create highly toxic wastes such as dioxin and other organochlorines.

The Environmental Protection Agency and many other public health agencies have found that dioxin (a by-product created when wood pulp is chlorine bleached) poses a cancer risk to humans and can have harmful effects on immune and reproductive systems of individuals.

You can help protect our air, water, and soil by requesting that the books you purchase be printed on chlorine-free recycled paper. In doing so, we both put our ecological values into actions that contribute to building a sustainable future–for our children, for generations to come, and for a healthy Earth home.

— *Errol G. Sowers*
Publisher